THE TEN COMMANDMENTS

Case Studies in Catholic Morality

THE TEN COMMANDMENTS

Case Studies in Catholic Morality

EILEEN P. FLYNN

ave maria press notre dame, indiana

Nihil Obstat: Reverend Michael Heintz
Censor Liborum

Imprimatur: Most Reverend John M. D'Arcy
Bishop of Fort Wayne-South Bend

Given at: Fort Wayne, Indiana, on 6 August 2009

The *Nihil Obstat* and *Imprimatur* are official declarations that a book or pamphlet is free of doctrinal or moral error. No implication is contained therein that those who have granted the *Nihil Obstat* or *Imprimatur* agree with its contents, opinions, or statements expressed.

Also by the Author:
Why Believe?: Foundations of Catholic Morality. Franklin, WI: Sheed & Ward, 2000.

©2010 by Ave Maria Press, Inc.

ISBN-10: 1-59471-223-9   ISBN-13: 978-1-59471-223-4

Project Editor: Michael Amodei

Cover image © jiunlimited.com

Cover design by Katherine Robinson Coleman.

Text design by John R. Carson.

Printed and bound in the United States of America.

CONTENTS

INTRODUCTION

✳ Morality and the Ten Commandments

orality is a complex subject, but comprehending it is important and necessary. A concise definition of morality is "knowledge based on human experience, reason, and God's revelation that discovers what we ought to be and what we ought to do to live fully human lives." Using the Ten Commandments, which were revealed by God and given to us as guidance for living our lives, we will examine how it is that God intends for us to live as morally good people. This is the subject of this book.

Making moral decisions impacts us in several ways, while in other choices morality does not matter. For example, whether or not it will rain, or even whether or not a friend will e-mail, are outcomes that are beyond people's abilities to determine. Therefore, it makes sense not to become invested in such matters and to try to take them in stride.

Or, it doesn't make much difference whether or not one chooses a sandwich or yogurt for lunch, or sleeps on a pillow or without a pillow. These, too, are trivial matters and have no ethical import.

Morality, however, is not a trivial matter, and it makes a great deal of sense to understand morality and to live in a morally upright manner. Applying the definition of morality further, we can say that morality entails doing the right thing and becoming a good person. Additionally, Catholic morality involves putting your faith and religion into practice through making good decisions in word and action. A morally good person perceives within himself or herself a sense of moral goodness that prompts a humble recognition that he or she is a worthy human being. The person has self-esteem and feels the peace of a good conscience.

A morally good person has every reason to be secure and happy. Morally good people engage in actions that promote human dignity; these are morally right actions. They reject actions that diminish human dignity, which are morally wrong. In addition, since morality impacts both individuals and the community, by their good actions, moral persons contribute to the well-being of society. God created humans to be morally good and to recognize and live by the moral standards that both God and human reason affirm. God wants people to share in his happiness and to enjoy the blessings that good conduct brings.

By consistently choosing to do the right thing, people distinguish themselves as moral persons. By habitually acting in a virtuous way, people develop integrity and the satisfaction of a life well lived. When faced with difficult problems, moral people can be counted on to thoughtfully consider what is at stake and to come to the right decision. Finally, positions that people take on the issues of our times, such as abortion, capital punishment, and racism, impact their moral identity. The sum total of these decisions—ethical positions and habits that characterize an individual as a morally good person—have a special kind of importance that is easy to recognize. When people decide, for example, to be truthful, respect life, and acknowledge God's dominion over creation, they feel secure and peaceful. On the other hand, if they are deceitful, disrespect life, and reject God's dominion, they can expect to be confused about the meaning of life and troubled by feelings of guilt.

God's Plan for Us

Many people nowadays make the mistake of thinking that they can make moral decisions based only on their personal opinions and feelings as well as on the laws imposed by the government. These same people often do not believe that there are objective and God-given laws and standards that they must follow in order to make good and moral decisions. People who think like this are wrong. They fail to recognize that God created humankind and that he has a plan for us; we have been entrusted with the work of perfecting ourselves and the rest of creation (*CCC*, 302). It is by our good actions that God intends that we complete his creation. It is God's will that good people work together to bring about a just and peaceful world. God anticipates that we will accomplish great good in our lives, "even those things which are yet to come into existence" (*CCC*, 302, quoting *Dei Filius*) through our morally good actions.

God created us to be happy in this life and, when we die, to share eternal happiness with God in Heaven. According to the divine plan, we will not be happy unless we strive to be morally good and live our lives doing good deeds and avoiding evil conduct.

Human persons have great dignity because we are created in the image and likeness of God. God is all-knowing, and humans, imaging God, possess reason, which makes us capable of understanding the order of things established by the Creator. The *Catechism of the Catholic Church* teaches that the desire for God is written in our hearts, and only in him will we attain the truth and happiness we desire (see *CCC*, 27). By our God-given free will we are capable of making correct moral choices. God intends us to grow into mature people by "seeking and loving what is true and good" (*CCC*, 1704).

God has given us an ability to determine what the right choice is in the many difficult situations life brings our way. This ability is called *conscience*, a practical judgment of reason that helps a person decide the goodness or sinfulness of an action or attitude. Moral conscience is present in the human heart, and it prompts people at the appropriate time to do good and to avoid evil. Conscience also judges particular choices, approving those that are good and denouncing those that are evil. Conscience bears witness to the authority of truth and recognizes God as the supreme good to whom human persons are drawn. Conscience welcomes the Ten Commandments because they contain directions for how to live our lives. When people listen to their consciences, they can hear God speaking.

In view of God's noble plan, why is it that individuals sometimes find themselves confused and unhappy? Why are their consciences troubled? Why are there crime and prejudice and selfishness in the world? These are important questions, and answering them requires that we consider how human misconduct undermines the plan of God.

The Reality of Sin

Sin, an offense against God through a violation of truth, reason, and conscience, is a dark reality that is present in all of our lives. The *Catechism* explains that "to try to understand what sin is, one must first recognize the profound relation of man to God, for only in this relationship is the evil of sin unmasked in its true identity as humanity's rejection of God and opposition to" the divine will (*CCC*, 386). When we sin, we act in immoral ways; we choose distorted ways of thinking and acting, and we prefer evil human tendencies to the moral structure established by God. Our sins lead to feelings of guilt and shame. For example, consider the many ramifications of cheating by students: cheating prevents the students themselves from learning, it sets a bad example for their classmates, it sabotages the honest work of teachers, and more.

Since sin hurts people individually and communally, why is it that sinful behaviors abound? Why doesn't humanity turn the page and start living without the harmful effects of sin?

Recall that sin is before all else an offense against God, a rupture of communion with God (*CCC*, 1440). God did not intend for humans to offend him. However, as the Judeo-Christian tradition holds, from the beginning of time humans sought through pride and willfulness to resist God's dominion and to suit themselves, rather than God. People foolishly thought that they knew better than their Creator. The story of Adam and Eve in the Book of Genesis makes this point. Adam and Eve, by disobedience, lost their closeness to God and their righteousness. Before they rebelled against God, they were happy and at peace, but after their acts of disobedience, they experienced shame and brokenness. This is called the Original Sin, that is the fallen state of human nature into which all generations of people are born. Christ Jesus came to save us from Original Sin. Yet, even though Jesus, through his Life, Death, Resurrection, and Ascension, restored humanity to God's favor, the effects of the sin of the first parents endure. The *Catechism* explains that this is the reality we live with:

> How did the sin of Adam become the sin of all his descendants? The whole human race is in Adam "as one body of one man." By this "unity of the human race" all men are implicated in Adam's sin, as all are implicated in Christ's justice. Still, the transmission of original sin is a mystery that we cannot fully understand. But we do know by Revelation that Adam had received original holiness and justice not for himself alone, but for all human nature. By yielding to the tempter, Adam and Eve committed a personal sin, but this sin affected the human nature that they would then transmit in a fallen state. It is a sin that will be transmitted by propagation to all mankind, that is, by the transmission of a human nature deprived of original holiness and justice. And that is why original sin is called "sin" only in an analogical sense: it is a sin "contracted" and not "committed"— a state and not an act. (*CCC*, 404)

You may need to read this excerpt a few times before its meaning becomes clear. The main ideas being communicated are first, that from the beginning humans have wanted to reject God's dominion, and second, the tendency to rebel is part of the reality of the human nature every individual possesses. Each one of us has been redeemed by Jesus and, through Baptism, shares Christ's life. But the pull of sin, inherited from Adam and Eve, exists alongside the grace of Christ.

Because human nature is a fallen nature, it is not a simple, easy matter to be a good person. St. Paul's words in the Letter to the Romans expresses the experience of people who fail in their resolutions to stop acting in sinful ways: "For I do not do the good I want, but the evil I do not want is what I do" (Rom 7:19). The fact that we are aware of our own sinfulness and that of others, however, should not result in pessimism or a decision to give up on becoming a good person. The reason to be optimistic is because the grace of Christ is stronger than Original Sin. With the help of Christ's grace, people can attain the goal of moral goodness. Just as students can eventually master the difficult subjects that they study, we can give up our sinfulness and work toward establishing societies that are just for all people. Jesus employed a parable to explain that good and evil exist side by side in the world, and he made the point that evil would exist until the end of time:

> The kingdom of heaven may be likened to a man who sowed good seed in his field. While everyone was asleep his enemy came and sowed weeds all through the wheat, and then went off. When the crop grew and bore fruit, the weeds appeared as well. The slaves of the householder came to him and said, "Master, did you not sow good seed in your field? Where have the weeds come from?" He answered, "An enemy has done this." His slaves said to him, "Do you want us to go and pull them up?" He replied, "No, if you pull up the weeds you might uproot the wheat along with them. Let them grow together until harvest; then at harvest time I will say to the harvesters, 'First collect the weeds and tie them in bundles for burning; but gather the wheat into my barn.'" (Mt 13:24–30)

The point of this parable is that there is evil and that God allows evil for his own reasons. Jesus said that evil will end in God's own time. It is important that we understand that the sinfulness we experience in ourselves and in society presents an obstacle to good conduct. This obstacle makes the quest for moral goodness difficult, and the existence of sin means that neither individuals nor societies will ever attain total moral goodness. Nevertheless, it is God's will that we reject sin and strive to do good and that we believe that God is with us, assisting with grace as we seek to do good and to achieve justice.

✳ God Reveals the Eternal Law and Natural Law

God, our Father, has endowed humans with the ability to reason. This means that by reasoning rightly we can know both the difference between good and bad actions and the wisdom of living life in accordance with God's will. The term for God's generosity to us in providing for what we need is *divine providence*, that is, God's leading and guiding us to our final end, salvation and union with him. *Eternal law* is the name for instruction from God that gives us insight into the ways that lead to happiness in this life and, in the end, the bliss of Heaven. God's eternal law also requires that we recognize and reject the ways of evil. Those preparing for the Sacrament of Confirmation learn that the Holy Spirit is the Guide who enables us to understand that only by right conduct can we live as God wants, and thus attain happiness and self-esteem. The *Catechism* makes this point when it says that "all law finds its first and ultimate truth in the eternal law. Law is declared and established by reason as a participation in the providence of the living God, Creator and Redeemer of all" (*CCC*, 1951).

Natural law is a system of moral reasoning that dates to the ancient Greeks. The philosopher Aristotle formulated the theory of natural law. Catholics understand natural law as the reasoned participation of humans in God's eternal law that reveals what he intends us to do and avoid according to his wise and loving plan. According to natural law, sane, mature individuals discover a reasoning process within themselves that is a tool for resolving moral dilemmas. (Very young children and mentally disabled individuals lack the capacity to reason correctly and hence are not able to reach rational moral judgments.)

A key to understanding natural law rests in the concept of *substantial form*. By substantial form it is meant that each specific category of being has a specific nature and can be counted on to act according to its nature. Thus, we expect dogs to bark, horses to gallop, and apples to grow on apple trees. This is because dogs, horses, and apple trees act in accordance with their natures or, in other words, conform to their substantial forms.

The substantial form of the human person differs radically from those of plants and animals. Plants follow the natures inscribed in them and animals act in accordance with their instincts. Humans are different. According to natural law, in their essence humans possess reason that allows them to act in conformity with their nature or go against their nature. Thus, humans can respond to hunger by eating or by continuing a hunger strike. They can satisfy a desire to acquire possessions by going on a shopping spree, or they can deprive themselves of this satisfaction and give money to a charitable cause. Human experience confirms that humans, by their substantial form, differ in fundamental ways from other beings. Thus, a key to natural law morality is to understand the roles human intellect and volition play for someone to become a morally good person.

By definition, natural law holds that persons have goals, for example, to be happy, complete, or good. With these goals in mind, the person should act in such ways as to bring about the desired results. Morally good deeds, consistently performed, will bring contentment or satisfaction or happiness. Another way to describe this action is "to become virtuous." By virtues, that is, good habits that help us to lead moral lives, people complete and perfect themselves. In the task of perfecting their nature, people perform morally good actions on a consistent, predictable basis. Their ease in performing these actions becomes second nature. The name for this predictability and ease is virtue.

The natural law approach to ethics is theoretically capable of yielding objective and measurable results because of the assumption that people will agree that what promotes human dignity and the well-being of society is morally good, and what retards dignity or the social order is morally objectionable. Also, fair-minded people will affirm the inherent soundness of this fact and formulate moral principles that are generally accepted. Natural law assumes that human reason will validate the premise that certain actions facilitate human development and are *morally good,* and other actions retard development and are *morally evil.*

Inevitably, in the course of life, people face moral dilemmas that require resolution. For example, a friend could ask that a lie be told to keep her from getting into trouble, or a banker could be asked to provide a loan to a customer who is a very poor credit risk, or a soldier could be ordered to bomb a civilian target. Moral dilemmas such as these put individuals on the spot and require that they make one decision or another.

Relying on the natural law for help in solving moral dilemmas is helpful. From the natural law methodology, lofty ideals and concepts have emerged. Justice, fairness, truthfulness, fidelity, respect, and a host of other ideals have consistently been advocated as morally mandatory. So have human rights and their correlative obligations. These insights, along with recognition of the fact that God requires morally correct choices, enable people facing dilemmas to arrive at the correct answers to their problems.

The Ten Commandments, the subject of this book, are a privileged expression of the natural law that teaches us the true humanity of the human person. The Catholic Church and the voice of moral conscience are in agreement that the Ten Commandments reveal the divine will for how humans should live and act.

The Ten Commandments in God's Revelation

The Ten Commandments, also referred to as the Decalogue, are considered to be "ten words" that point out the conditions of a life freed from sin. The Ten Commandments are derived from two books of the Old Testament, Exodus 20:2–17 and Deuteronomy 5:6–21. The commandments are part of God's Revelation because in them God makes his divine will known. The good deeds that humans do and the sinful conduct that they reject should constitute their moral response to God's invitation to be God's people. In fidelity to Scripture and in conformity with the example of Jesus, the Sacred Tradition of the Church has always acknowledged the importance of the Ten Commandments.

Jesus is the Revelation of God who walked among us and who taught us how to do the will of the Father. When asked by the rich young man what he needed to do to gain eternal life, Jesus answered, "If you would enter into life, keep the commandments" (Mt 19:16–17).

In his own life and in his teaching, Jesus cited obedience to the Ten Commandments as required for living according to God's will.

A covenant is a binding agreement between God and those who believe in him. Yahweh, the God of Israel, is a personal God who demands loyalty as well as for people to act in morally upright ways. In regard to the Old Covenant that Yahweh made with the Hebrew people, and which Jesus affirmed even while offering himself in a New Covenant relationship, the two sides are by no means equal. Believers who are bound to God in a covenant possess a sacred gift and should acknowledge the honor God has bestowed on them with humble gratitude.

The Ten Commandments state what is required of us in order to love God and love our neighbor. Jesus taught that our obligation to follow the Ten Commandments has not been removed or reduced. By grace, God makes it possible to keep the commandments. Furthermore, the Church contends that there is no conflict between the moral requirements of the Ten Commandments and the morality accessible to reason through the process of natural law reflection (see *CCC*, 2071). In other words, human reason is capable of affirming what the commandments tell us is right conduct. The human will, aided by God's grace, is capable of acquiring good habits and making morally correct choices. The commandments are a source to aid us in making good and moral choices and being good and moral people.

How to Use This Book

This text provides a synopsis of the meaning of each of the Ten Commandments. The opening section of each chapter defines the commandment, unpacks its theological meaning, and explains how it should be applied to one's everyday life.

The commandments themselves stir up moral debate, including the choice between right and wrong in many difficult situations. Each chapter offers several answers from a Catholic perspective to questions that are intimated by each commandment. These questions and answers are intended to help you both defend and apply the commandments to your everyday life.

Finally, for further clarification and application, three *case studies* are presented for each commandment. These case studies are drawn from a variety of simple to more complex moral dilemmas and require discernment to determine the correct and moral response for each. These case studies are suitable for personal reflection and further group interaction. Follow-up questions can likewise be used for both individual response (e.g., through journal writing) and for discussion among peers. The case studies also lend themselves to role-play and debate. With a group of classmates, consider enacting the case study prior to reflection and debate. Alternately, work with a panel of peers to discuss possible responses.

After all reflection, debate, and discussion, return to the introductory synopsis for the commandment as well as the questions and answers to gauge the moral correctness of your response according to Church teaching.

1ST COMMANDMENT

I am the Lord your God; you shall not have strange gods before me.

Synopsis

The first three commandments of the Decalogue focus on the love of humans for God. Jesus said, "You shall love the Lord your God with all your heart, and with all your soul, and with all your mind" (Mt 22:37). By obeying the first three commandments, we are able to demonstrate our total commitment to loving God.

The First Commandment specifically prohibits worship of false gods. In ancient times, pagan gods were various deities to whom tribes and nations paid homage. In contemporary times, things like money, sex, addictive substances, power, work, and even leisure activities can command as much attention as pagan gods once did. The First Commandment cautions against directing adoration toward anyone or anything other than the one, holy God. This commandment also reminds us to take seriously our duty to worship God and to bow down before his awesome holiness. Sins against the First Commandment include *idolatry* (worship of false gods), *atheism* (denial of God's existence), and *agnosticism* (the belief that no one knows for sure if God exists).

In observing the First Commandment, people manifest the theological virtues of faith, hope, and charity. The reference to pagan gods in the First Commandment may lead people to think that this commandment is not relevant today, and the idea that abiding by the First Commandment requires the practice of faith, hope, and charity may lead to the dismissive notion that there is not much required. Thinking like this would be wrong, as we can see from a recent tragic event that forced people to reexamine their faith and values.

On September 11, 2001, terrorists attacked the United States on four fronts. More than three thousand people were killed, and sorrow spread throughout the world. As the shock wore off and people struggled to move on, there was a lot of soul-searching in order to gain understanding about fundamental issues of good and evil. What does this tragic time have to do with the First Commandment? The United States Catholic Bishops answered that question in a pastoral letter titled *Living with Faith and Hope after September 11.* The bishops said that "our faith teaches us about good and evil, free will and responsibility," and they noted how, in the aftermath of the attacks, people turned to God in prayer. They went on to say that "hope assures us that, with God's grace, we will see our way through what now seems such a daunting challenge. For believers, hope is not a matter of optimism, but a source for strength and action in demanding times." Counseling Catholics to practice acts of charity and solidarity, the bishops indicated that faith, hope, and charity provide the foundation for recovery from the nightmare of September 11.

By practicing faith, hope, and charity, people fulfill the positive requirements of the First Commandment. And by rejecting despair, they open themselves to adopting a positive attitude that will allow them to cooperate in the task of building God's Kingdom on earth. With the virtue of faith one acknowledges that people have a duty to believe in God's goodness and to share their belief with others. We live in a secular society, and it is not easy to sustain our faith in God while living in a world where God's role and the requirements to follow him are seldom mentioned. Nevertheless, the First Commandment requires that we seek the support of family, friends, and the Church in strengthening our faith and rejecting anything that would undermine it.

The theological virtue of hope is manifest in "the confident expectation of divine blessing and the beatific vision of God; it is also the fear of offending God's love and of incurring punishment" (*CCC*, 2090). When people experience setbacks in life there is a tendency for them to lose hope, to become depressed, and to think in bleak terms about life. People commit the sin of despair when they cease to hope for personal salvation from God, for help in attaining it, or for the forgiveness of sins. An encouraging message contained in the First Commandment is that God's grace is with us, and the temptation to despair of God's grace is unfounded.

Just as there is no reason to despair, so there is no rational justification for being presumptuous. There are two kinds of presumption. Either people presume upon their own capacities, hoping to be able to save themselves without God's grace, or presume upon God's power or mercy and hope to obtain forgiveness without conversion and Heaven without merit.

The theological virtue of charity prompts us to acknowledge that God loves each of us and that we should love God above everything and love all creatures because he created them and because he loves them. It is possible to sin against the virtue of charity in several ways:

- by *indifference* we could live our lives as though we need never consider God's love and its power to transform our world;
- by *ingratitude* we could refuse to thank God for God's love and not direct our own love and gratitude to God;
- by *lukewarmness* we could be hesitant and negligent in responding to God's love;
- by *acedia*, that is, spiritual laziness or sloth, we could refuse to accept the joy that comes from God and even act as though we are repelled by divine goodness; and
- by the sin of *hatred* of God, which comes from pride, we could act contrary to love of God, whose goodness it denies. (*CCC*, 2094)

Someone who hates God lacks an understanding of the way life works: God sets limits with the commandments; God forbids sins; and God punishes unrepentant sinners. It makes no sense to hate God for

being God. On the contrary, it is completely reasonable to acknowledge and respect his dominion over us.

FAQs about the First Commandment

1. What does the First Commandment require that people do?

This commandment requires that God come first in one's heart and
mind; that his will and directions for human living be taken seriously
and not forgotten or brushed aside. God is God, holy, supreme, and
almighty. He requires the love and loyalty of all of his children. It
would be a grave mistake not to be totally humble before God.

2. Can a person be loyal to parents, siblings, friends, and classmates? Does God want to replace our affection to all of these others?

The issue is one of priorities and bringing oneself to the understanding that God is our Creator and loving Father and that he ought to
have first place in our lives. God wants each of us to live a full and
happy life and to have good relationships with all the people with
whom we interact. In addition, God wants to have first place in an
individual's affections and loyalty.

3. How can people be expected to love and trust an unseen God? We have no proof that God exists.

Creation, the awesome universe that we learn about in science and
whose wonders we witness on a daily basis, could not have come
into being without a First Cause. That First Cause is God, who is a
divine Spirit. Even though God is a pure Spirit who is not encoun-
tered in ways similar to how we encounter our parents or friends,
God is intimately connected with each and every person because
all of us are God's children. It makes a great deal of sense to love,

respect, and trust God who called each of us into being and who sustains all life on earth.

4. Does obedience to the First Commandment mean a person has to practice religion?

The *Catechism* tells us that "adoring God, praying to him, offering him the worship that belongs to him, and fulfilling the promises and vows made to him are acts of the virtue of religion which fall under obedience to the First Commandment" (*CCC*, 2135). God is our Father, and he wants his children to live their lives in relationship with him. This is a requirement, not an option, and is fulfilled through our participation in the Church.

5. How can seeking out money and sex for pleasure be considered "false gods"?

The First Commandment tells us to love God with all our hearts and not set our hearts on acquiring money or satisfying our appetites for sex and other pleasures. This is a different message from the popular media, including music lyrics, movie plots, television programming, and Internet blogs and social sites. The goal of life is not *hedonism*, that is, the satisfying of our desires for pleasure. Likewise, *narcissism*, the philosophy according to which everything revolves around the individual and life's main focus is what the individual desires, is a woefully inadequate basis for establishing the direction for your life. After we acknowledge that we should follow God's will and that we should offer him our deepest affection and loyalty, then we will be able to appreciate the fact that God wants us to have enough money to live comfortably and help others who have less. We will realize that God gave us our sexual appetites to enjoy within the context of marriage and that our sexuality has the dual purpose of uniting us with our husband or wife for life as well as bringing about the great blessing of children. Thus, money and sex are not goals in themselves but exist to enable us to live according to God's plan.

6. I have a friend who says he worships and prays to Satan. How can I help him to understand that this practice is wrong?

Satan is a fallen angel, a spirit who set itself up in opposition to God. Satan is not God; Satan is an enemy of God. To worship Satan would be a grave error because of two reasons: first, one would be worshipping an evil spirit and, second, one would be failing to acknowledge the true deity. Satan is only a creature. You may also wonder why God allows Satan to have any power, however fleeting, while we live on earth. The *Catechism,* quoting Romans 8:28, teaches that "it is a great mystery that providence should permit diabolical activity," but "we know that in everything God works for good with those who love him" (*CCC,* 395).

7. Is it wrong to carry good luck charms and to believe that having these items in one's possession will keep one safe and secure?

Wearing or carrying charms is against the spirit of the First Commandment because such a practice implies that the charm has the power to protect us from harm or bring us some advantage. More seriously, practices of magic by which one attempts to tame occult powers, so as to place them at one's service or manage them so the occult powers do not harm us, are contrary to the virtue of religion. These practices are even more to be condemned when accompanied by the intention of harming someone or when they have recourse to the intervention of demons.

8. What is *divination,* and why does it violate the First Commandment?

Divination is the act of foretelling future events or revealing occult knowledge by means of an alleged supernatural power. Practices such as "consulting horoscopes, astrology, palm reading, interpretation of omens . . . clairvoyance, and recourse to mediums" (*CCC,* 2116), such as those who claim to foretell the future or get in touch with the departed, are acts of divination. These practices are forbidden by the First Commandment because they express a human desire to have control over time, history, or other people. Since God is the all-knowing author of life, it would be sinful to try to access power that rightfully belongs to God.

9. What is *sacrilege,* and why is it forbidden by the First Commandment?

Sacrilege consists in disrespecting the sacraments and other liturgical actions, as well as persons, things, or places consecrated to God. Sacrilege is a grave sin especially when committed against the Eucharist, for in this sacrament the Body of Christ is made substantially present for us. It is very important for people to learn that books, objects, persons, and places considered sacred by Catholics, other Christians, and non-Christians should all be treated with respect.

10. What is *simony,* and why is it against the First Commandment?

Simony is defined as the buying or selling of spiritual things. The term comes from the name of Simon the Magician who attempted to buy spiritual powers from St. Peter (see Acts 8:9–25). The Catholic Church teaches that it is impossible to purchase or sell spiritual goods and behave toward them as their owner or master, for they have their source in God. One can receive these graces only from God. They are a gift from God; they do not require payment. Therefore, it would be wrong for an individual to approach a priest or a bishop and offer money to obtain the "grace of God." Likewise, it would be morally wrong for a religious authority to accept money from people and suggest or promise that the money will buy favor from God. Our loving Father loves each of us and wants to give blessings and graces to us. What God requires is that we be open to receiving his blessings and that we love and respect him. God's graces are not for sale.

11. Who are atheists and agnostics?

Atheism is a sin against the First Commandment. The word *atheism* comes from the Greek prefix *a* combined with the Greek word *theos,* and it literally means "there is no god." To assert that there is no god is the most fundamental error a person can make, and the consequence of thinking in this way is gravely deficient because humans would then consider themselves the highest level of beings and would be subject to no power greater than themselves. The eternal law of God would not be acknowledged or respected, and both individuals and society would suffer greatly as a result. It is also wrong to be an agnostic. An agnostic claims that a human person cannot know for certain that God exists because there is no tangible proof for God. Agnosticism is "a flight from the ultimate question of existence, and a sluggish moral conscience," and "agnosticism is all too often equivalent to practical atheism" (*CCC*, 2128). Therefore, agnosticism is likewise a sin against the First Commandment.

12. Is it wrong to pray to statues and holy pictures?

It is wrong to pray to statues and holy pictures as if they were gods. However, the *veneration* of sacred images is not contrary to the First Commandment. Jesus took on human flesh at his Incarnation and redeemed humans and all creation by his Death and Resurrection. By so doing, Jesus ennobled the human condition and concrete, material things that exist in our world share in the new order of creation. A statue, a crucifix, a religious picture, or a fresco in a cathedral, is a material object that has been crafted to remind people of God's role in our lives and our religious history. Holy images include statues and pictures depicting Mary, the Mother of God, angels, saints, and holy people of the Bible. These statues and images are not God, and they do not have magic powers; they are in place to remind us of God and his role in our lives. As the *Catechism* explains, "Religious worship is not directed to images in themselves, considered as mere things, but under their distinctive aspect as images leading us on to God incarnate. The movement toward the image does not terminate in it as image, but tends toward that whose image it is" (*CCC*, 2132 [In this paragraph the *Catechism* relies on the medieval writing of St. Thomas Aquinas: *Summa Theologica*, II–II, 81, 3 *ad* 3]).

CASE STUDY:
Chain Letter

Caroline is a high school junior who is busy with school and extra-curricular activities, including cheerleading and working on the yearbook. She attends Mass regularly and takes her faith seriously in all ways. Lately, Caroline has been feeling very stressed because her paternal grandmother had a stroke and is in the hospital. She is partially paralyzed and has trouble speaking. The doctors cannot say how much functioning she might recover, and Caroline and her family are worried. Caroline wishes there were something she could do to help her grandmother get better.

When Caroline logs on to her laptop on a Saturday morning, she sees an e-mail message from an unfamiliar sender and, out of curiosity, she opens it. The message is a chain letter that instructs Caroline to make a wish and then to say a prayer nine times a day for nine days; to forward the e-mail to nine friends, asking them to do likewise; and to expect great joy on the tenth day.

The words of the prayer are attributed to a saint and the words are: "Holy God, merciful and true, behold your servant in her hour of need and grant her humble request in Jesus' name. Amen." Caroline has no way of finding out whether or not the saint actually formulated the prayer, or whether it was made up by the unknown sender.

The e-mail assures Caroline that many people have already received blessings as a result of following the directions. However, the letter also contains a warning that if the recipient deletes the e-mail and does not follow the directions, her wishes will not come true, and bad things will happen.

Caroline is troubled because she wants to believe that by doing what the letter outlines, saying the stipulated prayer and encouraging her friends to do so, too, she can get God to make her grandmother better. However, she has learned in her religion class that God cannot be manipulated into doing things that people want and that superstitious practices are against the First Commandment. Feeling torn and confused, Caroline prints the e-mail and takes it to her dad. She is going to ask his help before making a decision.

EVALUATION

1. Have you ever received a chain letter? What have you done with it?
2. What do you think Caroline's father is going to tell her to do about the letter?
3. What can Caroline do to help her grandmother at this difficult time?
4. The First Commandment suggests that God is supreme and that humans should subordinate themselves to God's dominion or rule. In this case, how does God's rule apply?

CASE STUDY:
Modern Day Idolatry

Jonathan is beginning his freshman year at a community college. The downturn in the economy has had a bad effect on his family, and the money his parents expected to have for his tuition, room, and board at a four-year school disappeared several months ago when their investments lost value. Jonathan is very unhappy that he is not able to live at and attend his "dream school." His unhappiness is affecting him in many ways.

Before things became difficult for his family, Jonathan loved English literature, and his goal had been to teach that subject in either high school or college. Now Jonathan finds himself obsessed by the idea of pursuing courses that will lead to a higher-paying job. He wants to make and save a lot of money so that he will have cash to buy anything he wants. Jonathan assumes that someday he will marry and have children, and he wants to have money in the bank and in sound investments so that his children never have to readjust their dreams because of financial hardship.

Jonathan's parents observe that he is changing; he is sullen and impatient, not optimistic like he used to be. Jonathan talks a lot about taking courses that will open career doors, and he pays much more attention to internship options in business fields than they ever thought he would. When they ask why he has changed his mind about studying English literature, Jonathan becomes surly and says that he doesn't want to talk about it.

Jonathan also stops going to Mass and does not join the family in grace before meals. When his parents ask him why he is neglecting religious practices, he comments that God does not care about the predicament he is in, so why should he waste his time on God. "Money," Jonathan says, "that's what is important. You can see and taste and experience what it will buy. Who knows if the God you pray to even exists. And, if God does exist, then why doesn't God take care of us?"

EVALUATION

1. What kinds of spiritual and emotional problems does Jonathan manifest?
2. Jonathan thinks that money is most important, and he decides to concentrate on trying to get as much as he can. How important is money, and how much effort is appropriate for someone to acquire it?
3. Based on what you know of the First Commandment, what suggestions would you make to Jonathan about his current state of mind?
4. Jonathan's parents are troubled by the changes in their son. What might they do to help him at this difficult time?

CASE STUDY:
Practice of Religion

S amantha and Kevin are planning to tell their parents that they are engaged and that they plan to marry within a year or two. They are in their mid-twenties, have started careers, have a lot in common, and believe that they are in love. They think that their parents will be pleased by their decision to marry, especially since they plan to marry in a Catholic church.

Both Samantha and Kevin were raised in the Catholic faith, but neither has practiced the religion since high school. Samantha longs to return to Mass and has begun to pray again. Kevin says that he does not miss anything about religion and that he is not even convinced that God exists. He thinks that religions are all pretty much the same and, even though he was brought up in the Catholic faith, he feels no attraction to it. At the same time, he does not want to upset either set of parents, and he is willing to go to church with Samantha because religion is an aspect of life that she feels is important.

Kevin tells Samantha that he will just be going through the motions; she tells him that she thinks that if he starts to go to church with her and tries to pray, he may begin to reconnect with God and the Catholic faith. Samantha also knows that by attending Mass regularly, they will have a better chance of being able to have their wedding in a Catholic church with a priest as witness.

Before breaking their news to their parents, Kevin thinks it important that they rehearse what they are going to say about religion. He tells Samantha that the best course is just to say, "We've started going to church, and we plan to marry in church." Let their parents assume that Samantha and he are on the same page. There's no reason to explain the situation further, and there is good reason to hope that parental approval will lead to no other questions.

EVALUATION

1. Do you think it would be wrong for Kevin to attend Mass with Samantha even though he professes no faith? Why or why not?

2. Samantha cares about religion and wants to start going to Mass regularly. She also plans to marry Kevin. Does it matter that he does not share her religious convictions? How could Kevin's lack of faith cause problems for their marriage?

3. How likely is Kevin to "get religion" by sitting next to Samantha at Mass?

4. Comment on what you think prompts Samantha's and Kevin's parents to want their children to marry in church as well as the way Kevin proposes to tell them about their plans.

2ND COMMANDMENT

You shall not take the name of the Lord, your God, in vain.

Synopsis

The spirit of the Second Commandment requires much more of a person than not committing perjury or not using God's name in an offensive way. This commandment encourages us to acknowledge God's dominion over us and all creation so that we live our lives as humble, reverent people. The commandment directs us to bless, praise, and glorify God's name, and tells us how to speak without offending him.

Sins especially to be avoided are irreverent use of God's name, blasphemy, perjury, misusing God's name in oaths, and taking false oaths. People tend to pick up bad habits and then to make excuses for why these habits are not a big deal. For example, we frequently hear people use God's name when expressing surprise ("Oh, my G-d"), disagreement ("G-d, no"), or disapproval or impatience ("G-d damn"). You may even say such things yourself. The ordinariness and frequency of such speech does not change the fact that it displeases God and is forbidden by the Second Commandment.

Blasphemy is a sin directly opposed to the Second Commandment. It consists in uttering words of hatred, reproach, or defiance against God; in speaking ill of God; in failing to show respect toward God in one's speech; or in misusing God's name. To misuse the holy name of Jesus is blasphemy. Blasphemy also extends to language against Christ's Church, the saints, and sacred things. It is also blasphemous to make use of God's name to cover up criminal practices, to torture persons, or to put them to death. The misuse of God's name in committing a crime can provoke others to repudiate religion.

The Second Commandment also forbids taking false oaths ("I swear to G-d"). This is because taking an oath, or swearing, is to take God as witness to what one affirms. In taking an oath, a person invokes the divine truthfulness as a pledge of one's own truthfulness. Obviously, it would be a sinful distortion to call upon God to witness an untruth.

FAQs about the Second Commandment

1. What does the Second Commandment require that people do?

The Second Commandment requires that people think before they speak and come to appreciate the importance of expressing themselves as reverent and truthful persons. In negative terms, this commandment requires that people not dishonor or misuse God's holy name, the name of Jesus; the names of Mary, the Mother of God; and the saints. This commandment also requires that people cultivate an attitude of reverence toward God, Mary, and all of the saints. Jesus said that it is not what goes into a person's mouth that defiles the person, but, rather what comes out (cf. Mt 15:11). We are to perfect ourselves. One very important aspect of doing so is to regulate speech so that it is reverent toward God.

2. What is a false oath and why are false oaths considered sinful?

A false oath calls on God to be witness to a lie. "Rejection of false oaths is a duty toward God. As Creator and Lord, God is the norm of all truth. Human speech is either in accord with or in opposition to God who is Truth itself. When it is truthful and legitimate, an oath highlights the relationship of human speech with God's truth" (*CCC*, 2151). A false oath totally undermines this relationship.

3. Why is swearing forbidden by the Second Commandment?

In colloquial speech, swearing has two meanings. According to the first meaning, a person mentions the name of God in the form of an oath, but in the context of a trivial matter in which there is no need to call on God to witness to the person's veracity. For example, a person might say something such as, "I swear to G-d I didn't hear my cell phone ring." It is unnecessary to "swear to G-d" in such a situation, and such usage would be against the spirit of the Second Commandment. People should exercise discretion in calling upon God and not be disrespectful by asking him to verify their truthfulness in matters that are unimportant. A second meaning of swearing is uttering obscene expressions, usually when experiencing surprise or something that causes angry feelings. These words are offensive and are termed "expletives" by those unwilling to repeat them. This type of swearing, while not forbidden by the Second Commandment, gives evidence of a coarsening or irreverence that runs counter to cultivating the habit of self-control.

4. Is it permissible to take oaths in casual circumstances, or should oaths only be taken on solemn occasions, as in court proceedings?

St. Ignatius of Loyola, a medieval saint and the founder of the Jesuit religious order, answered this question centuries ago when he said, "Do not swear whether by the Creator, or any creature, except truthfully, of necessity, and with reverence" (*CCC*, 2164). The reason to be reluctant to swear is that in so doing we are explicitly calling on God to witness the truth of what we say, and we should only do this in the exceptional and necessary circumstances where we are legally obliged to do so. In all other circumstances, we should speak truthfully, aware that we are in the presence of God and that he intends that we always tell the truth.

5. **Is it permissible to lie under oath in a court proceeding for a very important reason, such as to protect a loved one or to prevent something bad from happening?**

No, it is not permissible to lie under oath for any reason. A person who takes an oath in a legal situation promises to "tell the truth, the whole truth, and nothing but the truth." The person makes this promise with his or her hand on a Bible, implying that God is witness to the truth of what is being said. Having made such an explicit declaration, it would be morally wrong to state a falsehood as though it were the truth.

6. **Why do Catholics begin their prayers "In the name of the Father, and of the Son, and of the Holy Spirit"?**

The invocation, "In the name of the Father, and of the Son, and of the Holy Spirit," is the way Catholics begin their days, prayers, and activities. Baptized people dedicate the day to the glory of God and call on the Savior's grace, which lets them act in the Spirit as children of the Father. The Sign of the Cross strengthens us to resist temptations and persevere in the face of difficulties. By prayerfully blessing ourselves with the Sign of the Cross, we affirm the relationship we have with the Triune God.

7. **Some people are casual in the way they use God's name; they have been brought up hearing family members speak this way, and they have picked up this practice. They mean no harm by it. Is it morally wrong for them to utter the words "God" and "Jesus" in an offhand way?**

Yes, it is wrong to engage in careless use of the names of God, Jesus, Mary, and the saints. If people do this out of an unconscious habit they acquired as children and do not intend to be disrespectful toward God, their fault would fall in the category of venial sin. It would be a mistake, however, to excuse oneself of this type of failing and think that it is *only* a venial sin. Since such a way of speaking violates the Second Commandment, this bad habit should be broken, and people should endeavor to speak only in reverent ways about God.

8. **It can be hard to fit in with a group if you do not talk the way the others do. Wouldn't God understand if people cursed occasionally so as to fit in? After all, they mean God no disrespect.**

Cursing is manifest in many forms or speech: it happens when one wishes evil or misfortune on someone, frequently invoking God to bring the desired harm; or when a person uses profane words or phrases. God may understand why people misbehave by cursing, but this does not mean that people should offend God by cursing. If an individual needs to choose between fitting into a group whose members do not manifest respect for God and rejecting membership in such a group, the individual should refuse to join the group. The First Commandment instructs us that our first priority should be to be on good terms with God. The Second Commandment requires that we do not take the name of the Lord in vain. These commandments are part of the eternal law of God, and they are not open to negotiation. Neither do the commandments allow humans to disregard them when following them is difficult.

9. **Why does the Catholic Church teach that infants who are baptized in the Catholic faith should receive a saint's name?**

The Sacrament of Baptism is conferred "in the name of the Father and of the Son, and of the Holy Spirit." In Baptism, the Lord's name sanctifies us, and parents declare their child's name to the Church. The name should be of a saint, that is, of a person who has lived a life of exemplary fidelity to the Lord. The patron saint provides a model of charity, and as people go through their lives, they come to rely on their patron saint to intercede for them before the throne of God. The baptismal name can also express a Christian mystery or Christian virtue. Giving a child a Christian name is so important that "parents, sponsors, and the pastor are to see that a name is not given which is foreign to Christian sentiment" (CCC, 2156).

CASE STUDY:
Profanity in a Motion Picture

Rob and Laura are planning to double-date with friends. Their friends live in the neighborhood; they are not Catholic and, in fact, they do not belong to any religion. The friends suggest that they go to a new movie. They claim that it is funny, action-packed, and really hot. Tentative plans are made to attend the movie on Saturday night.

When they are alone, Rob mentions to Laura that he has heard about this movie from other acquaintances and that he knows that it is full of profanity. Most people consider the use of profane language funny or appropriate because it is matched to situations, but, from what he has heard, the words "God" and "Jesus" come up frequently in very irreverent ways. Rob knows that Laura finds it offensive to hear God's name used in a casual or disparaging way, and he, too, feels uncomfortable about profanity. He asks her whether or not she thinks they should go through with the upcoming date.

Laura says that she definitely does not want to patronize the movie, but she is unsure about how to handle the situation. She says that the way she sees it, they have two choices: tell their friends that something has come up and that they cannot join them on Saturday evening; or explain that they have moral objections to the misuse of God's name in the movie and that they do not want to patronize it.

EVALUATION

1. Which course do you think Rob and Laura should follow: making an excuse about why they can't go to the movie, or explaining how they feel about profanity? Why do you feel this way?

2. There is a lot of irreverence toward God's name in motion pictures and in everyday life. Does following the Second Commandment require that people confront this irreverence, or is it enough for them to only watch how they speak?

3. If Rob and Laura do go to the movie, how should they act when the Lord's name is taken in vain?

CASE STUDY:
Blasphemous Thoughts

J oshua's thoughts are troubling him. He is a high school junior whose parents recently divorced, and he has moved to a new town and now attends a new school. Joshua's parents share custody, and he is having difficulty adjusting to the changed situation of his life. He feels lonely and insecure and is frequently angry and depressed. When Joshua is down, he finds himself thinking negatively of God and thinking things like, "G-d damn my life; G-d damn my school; G-d damn my classmates; G-d damn my parents."

Joshua's thoughts alarm him. He has been brought up to keep the commandments, and he knows that the Second Commandment is "You shall not take the name of the Lord, your God, in vain." He is unhappy with himself, and he is also confused. He does not actually say out loud the words he is thinking; they are either in his mind or formed by his lips. Sometimes he thinks that he is violating the commandment; sometimes he thinks that he is not violating it.

Joshua is conflicted within himself, and he does not know whether or not the sentiments that keep occurring to him need attending to. On one hand, he wants to rationalize and believe that he is not breaking any law of God, but, on the other hand, he feels uneasy about the fact that he is angry and that he seems to be reproaching God for the instability in his life.

EVALUATION

1. When Joshua thinks and mouths "G-d damn," is he violating the Second Commandment? Explain.
2. How could negative and angry thoughts about God lead Joshua to immoral actions? What is the connection between what is in someone's mind and what that person does?
3. Given the trying situation Joshua finds himself in, what kinds of things can he do to get to a better place in his mind and in his heart?

CASE STUDY:
To Lie Under Oath

Aaron Cassidy is a high school math teacher. He is also a home-room teacher and, in this capacity, Mr. Cassidy is responsible for taking attendance every day and for keeping attendance records.

Jamie is a student in Mr. Cassidy's homeroom who confided in his teacher that his father had lost his job and that there is rarely any food in his home to feed him and his siblings. "I don't care for myself, Mr. Cassidy," Jamie said. "But a five-year-old and eight-year-old should have three square meals per day." Mr. Cassidy asked Jamie if his parents had applied for government aid and whether they were aware of several food pantries in the community to help out those in need. Jamie told Mr. Cassidy that his father had made an announcement to the family just the night before: "We will never accept charity of any kind."

Nevertheless, Mr. Cassidy took steps to report the situation to school administrators. In the meantime, Jamie was absent from school for three consecutive days. When he returned, he told Mr. Cassidy that he had been arrested for breaking into the snack bar at the local sports complex and accused of stealing over $1,000. Because he is over eighteen, Jamie will be tried as an adult.

Jamie has a public defender who brings the case to trial. The attorney summons Mr. Cassidy to be a witness for his case. Mr. Cassidy agrees and is sworn in. After several questions about Jamie's character, the lawyer asks Mr. Cassidy if he knows of any reason Jamie would have for stealing. Mr. Cassidy does know a reason, but he thinks if he answers truthfully, his testimony could be damning. Jamie would probably get probation, but his family might also have to cough up court fees and a fine. If they can't afford to do so, there may be a chance Jamie would have to spend some time in the county jail.

EVALUATION

1. How do you think Mr. Cassidy should answer the question about whether or not Jamie had a reason to steal?
2. Mr. Cassidy believes that Jamie could not have committed the robbery because he knows Jamie and he does not believe Jamie could have done such a thing. Assuming that Mr. Cassidy is correct, what should he do to help him?
3. Is it ever morally permissible to lie under oath?

3RD COMMANDMENT

Remember to keep holy the Lord's Day.

Synopsis

For Catholics and all Christians, Sunday is regarded as the Lord's Day, a day in which they are required to keep the day holy by participating at Mass and avoiding unnecessary work. People tend to be casual about both parts of this commandment, either irregularly attending Mass and/or engaging in chores, work, or social events that take away from time with God and family. This is a mistake. At a minimum, as far as possible, manual labor or working for money should not occupy Christians on Sunday because these pursuits prevent people from spending Sunday as God intends. And how does God intend that the Lord's Day be kept? The key to answering this question is to understand that the focus of the Lord's Day should be on developing one's spiritual relationship with God. Accordingly, celebrating the Eucharist, spending time in spiritual reading and prayer, and joining in family activities should be stressed. There should be a break from the study, work, and stress of the rest of the week so that the concerns of one's spiritual life become a priority.

It is true that young people are busy and that their lives are full and often hectic. They want time for themselves and space to deal with things that are important to them. Making time for God on Sunday should not be seen as a useless burden or a chore they cannot get out of. On the contrary, making time for God is the first essential step to take in establishing a relationship with God. By opening your heart to God on Sunday, you allow God to be present in your life and to influence your thinking and your choices. The light of God's love brings peace, and the closeness of God brings happiness. Time devoted to the spiritual life is time well spent, and it enables people to grasp what is important and put the rest of one's activities in perspective.

FAQs about the Third Commandment

1. Why do Jews observe the Sabbath on Saturday and Christians the Lord's Day on Sunday?

The word *sabbath* has Hebrew and Greek origins, and it means "to rest" or "to cease work." The first story of Creation in the Book of Genesis recounts that God created the world in six days, and on the seventh day he rested. We read, "On the seventh day God finished the work that he had done, and he rested on the seventh day from all the work that he had done. So God blessed the seventh day and hallowed it, because on it God rested from all the work that he had done in creation" (Gn 2:2–3). In obeying the Third Commandment, the Chosen People rested from work and prayed on the Sabbath, which they observed weekly on the seventh day, from sunset Friday until sunset on Saturday. Christians modified Jewish practice by observing the Lord's Day from sunset Saturday until sunset on Sunday. The reason for this change is that Jesus rose from the dead on Sunday, and believers established the practice of meeting on Sunday to celebrate the Life, Death, Resurrection, and Ascension of Jesus. From the writings of St. Ignatius of Antioch, a second-century bishop, we learn that followers of Christ observed rest on Sunday beginning in the very early history of the Church: "Those who lived according to the old order of things have come to a new hope, no longer keeping the sabbath, but the Lord's Day, in which our life is blessed by him and by his death" (Ignatius of Antioch quoted in *CCC*, 2174).

2. Why does God require attendance at Mass on Sundays?

God requires that people who believe in God and are in relation-ship with Jesus maintain that relationship and express that belief. Remember that the first three commandments of the Decalogue require that believers love God with their whole heart. Love for God is rightly expressed in the communal prayer of the Eucharist. The *Catechism* explains why the Church requires that believers attend Mass on Sunday: "Participation in the communal celebration of the Sunday Eucharist is a testimony of belonging and of being faithful to Christ and to his Church. The faithful give witness by this to their communion in faith and charity. Together they testify to God's holiness and their hope of salvation. They strengthen one another under the guidance of the Holy Spirit" (*CCC*, 2182). Attendance at Sunday Mass is also one of the precepts of the Church. Deliberately missing Mass on Sunday or on a holy day of obligation is an occa-sion of mortal sin.

3. Why are Catholics supposed to go to Mass *every* Sunday? Wouldn't it be enough to go most Sundays?

This question contains an underlying complaint that going to Mass weekly is too much to ask of a Catholic. This type of complaint is unfortunate because it reveals confusion about the real nature and beauty of the celebration of the Eucharist. Sunday is a holy day, the day the Lord has made, and Catholics are blessed because they have the opportunity to express their religious identity at Mass and renew their covenant with God. If people were really honest, they would admit that it is not easy to maintain a relationship with Jesus by going to Mass *only* once a week, and they would begin to incorporate spiritual practices such as prayer and reading the Bible into their weekday lives to supplement the communal worship of Sunday Mass.

4. How can I experience Mass as less boring?

The reason Mass seems boring to some people is because they do not understand what is happening or because they allow themselves to be distracted and do not participate. You can also make the Mass less boring if you come to participate with a good and right attitude.

The Mass is the prayer of the Church in which the faithful recall the teachings of Jesus; reflect on their meaning; offer the bread and wine to God; receive Jesus in the Eucharist; and unite their prayers and their regrets for their sins with Catholics all over the world. These spiritual acts fortify and deepen them in faith; they are not boring, and there is no substitute for them.

5. Does watching Mass on television count as fulfilling my Sunday obligation?

If people are unable to get to church because of illness, the need to take care of a sick family member or an infant, bad weather, lack of transportation, or the requirements of work, they do well to watch Mass on television. This medium brings the ritual to the individual's home, but, unfortunately, the individual is not able to participate with others or to receive the Eucharist. Occasionally and for reasons like those mentioned above, watching Mass on television is acceptable, but people should make the effort to attend Mass in church on a regular basis.

6. Is anyone excused from the obligation to attend Mass on Sunday?

People are excused from the obligation to attend Sunday Mass if they are traveling, working, or sick on Sunday and, therefore, find it impossible for them to attend. In addition, severe weather conditions can prevent people from traveling to church, and family emergencies can occasionally present a valid excuse for not attending Mass.

7. If Catholics do not go to Mass on Sunday, do they commit a sin?

Yes, if Catholics deliberately miss Mass on a Sunday (or holy day of obligation), it is an occasion of sin. Failing to pray and failing to keep holy the Lord's Day are also occasions of sin.

8. **In the United States there is a priest shortage and projections are that it will get worse. What should Catholics do if there is no priest to preside at Mass in their area?**

The *Catechism of the Catholic Church* responds: "If because of lack of a sacred minister or for other grave cause participation in the celebration of the Eucharist is impossible, it is specially recommended that the faithful take part in the Liturgy of the Word if it is celebrated in the parish church or in another sacred place" (*CCC*, 2183). The Liturgy of the Word is comprised of the prayers and readings for each Sunday and contained in a book called the *Lectionary*. Two readings, one from the Old Testament and one from the New Testament, precede the reading of an excerpt from one of the four Gospels. At Mass, the Liturgy of the Word is one of two major parts; the other is the Liturgy of the Eucharist. Obviously, the fact that there is a priest shortage in the United States Catholic Church should prompt young people to think about what steps they might take to address this problem and resolve it. If you are male, you should consider a vocation to the priesthood. All Catholics should make it their responsibility to pray for more priestly vocations.

9. **After attending Mass on Sunday, how should people spend the rest of the day? Is it a sin to go shopping or play sports on Sunday? What about attending sporting events and other kinds of entertainment?**

Two things to keep in mind are that believers need to devote time to their relationship with God and that they also need to cultivate the familial, cultural, and social aspects of their lives. It is not sinful to shop, participate in sports, and attend sporting events or other kinds of entertainment on Sunday, but it would be a mistake not to make spiritual and family interests a priority.

10. **Does the Third Commandment prohibit every kind of work on Sunday?**

The Third Commandment allows people to do necessary tasks such as cooking meals and making beds. Yard work and house painting would be better left for other days, and work for pay, if possible, should not be performed on Sunday. However, Jesus said, "The sabbath was made for man, not man for the sabbath; so the Son of Man is lord even of the sabbath" (Mk 2:27–28). This statement was made in response to Pharisees who criticized Jesus and his followers for picking grain on the sabbath. The point here is that we need to recognize the religious requirement to devote time to nurturing our relationship with God, and we should not worry about doing necessary things that fall into the category of work.

11. Many commercial and municipal activities occur on Sunday. Is it permissible to hire people to work on Sunday, and how much time off should they be given to attend religious services?

A common effort is needed to ensure that Sunday remains a day of rest, and Christians should avoid making unnecessary demands on others that would hinder them from observing the Lord's Day. Traditional activities, such as attending sporting events or eating in restaurants, and civil necessities, such as providing public transportation and police patrols, require some people to work on Sundays. Police, fire, and medical personnel are also necessary and required to work on Sundays. Public authorities should ensure that public employees receive time for worship and rest, and private employers should do likewise for their employees.

12. In the United States there are holy days of obligation on which Catholics are supposed to go to Mass. Why does the Church add these days to the Sunday requirement?

The bishops of the United States decided in 1991 to reaffirm Catholic tradition and require that Catholics observe six holy days a year by attending Mass and, if possible, refraining from work or school. The reason for observing these six holy days is to keep Catholics mindful of great feasts that have been celebrated in the Church for centuries. These six holy days are: January 1, the Solemnity of Mary, Mother of God; Thursday of the Sixth Week of Easter, the Solemnity of the Ascension; August 15, the Solemnity of the Assumption of the Blessed Virgin Mary; November 1, the Solemnity of All Saints; December

8, the Solemnity of the Immaculate Conception; and December 25, the Solemnity of the Nativity of Our Lord Jesus Christ. Whenever January 1, the Solemnity of Mary, Mother of God, or August 15, the Solemnity of the Assumption, or November 1, the Solemnity of All Saints, falls on a Saturday or on a Monday, there is no obligation to attend Mass depending on the wishes of the local bishop.

CASE STUDY:
Ten O'clock Mass

arah is a Catholic who made her Confirmation last year and whose parents and teachers expect her to practice her religion by attending Mass and developing a lively spiritual life. Lately Sarah has found going to Mass boring, and she feels that people are putting too much pressure on her to pray and go to church. Some of her friends have stopped attending Mass. Sarah wonders why she is the "only" one who has to wake up on Sunday morning or even "waste" a Saturday evening to go to Mass.

Sarah's parents usually expect her to go to the ten o'clock Mass on Sunday morning with them; it is a family exercise, and her participation is not open to discussion. Sarah lives in their house, and she is expected to follow their rules. It happens, however, that an emergency involving a grandparent necessitates that Sarah's mom and dad be away from home on Sunday morning. Before they leave, they tell Sarah not to wait for them and to go to Mass by herself.

Sarah thinks about the options the change in circumstances opens up. She can go to Mass by herself and just sit there daydreaming. Or, she can stop at the church, pick up a bulletin in the vestibule, and take a walk. The only problem with the second option is that her mom and dad may start asking her what the homily was about, and she might be clueless.

EVALUATION

1. What do you think about Sarah's parents' expectations that she go to Mass every Sunday?
2. What do you do if and when you find Mass to be boring?
3. Because she finds Mass boring, Sarah thinks about taking a bulletin and pretending that she was at Mass. What steps could Sarah take to deal with her boredom and reenergize herself so that attending Mass will become a meaningful experience for her?
4. Does God care whether or not Sarah goes to Mass?

CASE STUDY:
No Time for Mass on Sunday

K atie, a sixteen-year-old Catholic, gets a job as a live-in *au pair* for the summer. She babysits two preschoolers; one is eighteen months, and the other is four years old. The children's parents, who do not belong to any religion, own a restaurant that serves Sunday brunch, and they work every Sunday morning. Saturday nights are always busy at the restaurant, too, so Katie's days off are in the middle of the week.

When she started her job, Katie did not think about not being able to get to Mass but, after a few weeks of not going to church, she missed being there and decided to ask her employers to make arrangements so that she could have time Saturday evening or Sunday morning to attend Mass. They were surprised by her request and told her that they would think about it and get back to her.

A few days later Katie's employers tell her that they can not accommodate her. They say that they pay her well and that they let her know before she started working for them that her days off would be during the week. There are seven weeks left in the summer, and they are sure that God can wait until September to see her in church. They work hard to earn money to support themselves, and they expect loyalty and understanding from Katie and their other employees.

EVALUATION

1. Do employers—including non-Christian employers—have a responsibility to provide opportunities for employees to attend religious services? Why or why not?
2. Is Katie's request a reasonable one, or is she asking too much?
3. Given the fact that her employers are unwilling to accommodate her needs, what should Katie do?
4. Katie's employers depend on Saturday night and Sunday morning customers for a considerable share of their income. Katie needs to meet both her responsibilities to her employers

and her obligation to worship God. Which duty should be her priority? Why?

CASE STUDY:
Sunday, the Day to Relax

Justin thinks that Sunday is meant for relaxing. He understands that some people go to Mass on Sunday and spend time in spiritual reading and family activities, and he has no problem with this. But, in his opinion, what a person does on a day off is up to that person, and there should be no pressure placed on anyone to pray, or go to church, or anything like that.

Justin attends a Catholic high school. At the end of the semester, one of the evaluation questions asks students to state any issues that they think need to be brought to the attention of the faculty and administration. Students participate in the evaluation process anonymously.

Justin writes: "I believe Sunday is a day to relax. For me, relaxing means sleeping late, playing sports, listening to music, being online, hanging out with friends, and maybe watching some TV. I have to get up early all week to get to school, and homework takes up my time later in the day. On Saturdays, I have chores in the house and yard. Sunday is the only day I have for myself. I find it annoying that my teachers assume that every Catholic teen should go to Mass on Sunday, like this is something that kids need to do. I don't need or want to attend Mass or say prayers, so I wish the faculty would act like this is the twenty-first century."

EVALUATION

1. Who does Justin assume Sunday exists for? Why does he make this assumption?
2. How many of your peers regularly participate at Sunday Mass? For one friend who does go to Mass, tell why he or she does. For one friend who does not go to Mass, explain why you think this is so.
3. Evaluate Justin's method of protest. Would it have been preferable for him to speak up during class rather than to keep his

dissatisfaction to himself until the end of the semester? Why or why not?

4TH COMMANDMENT

Honor your father and your mother.

Synopsis

The Fourth Commandment begins the portion of the Decalogue that addresses the second half of the Great Commandment given to us by Jesus, "You shall love your neighbor as yourself" (Mt 19:19). Historically, the Fourth Commandment was intended to remind adult children of their responsibility to take care of their aging parents. The spirit of the Fourth Commandment suggests that children of all ages owe respect, gratitude, obedience, and assistance to their parents. Parents are required to nurture and educate their children, to provide religious instruction and good example. The family is the foundational unit of society; within the home parents and children should live according to Christian values so that they will know how to exercise these values outside the home.

The family is society's foundational unit. The family supports the love of a husband and a wife, the procreation of children, and the religious growth and education of children as responsible members of the human family. God's plan for the family calls for parents and children to experience worth and dignity and fundamental equality as people with rights, and to learn how to exercise those rights and relate to others responsibly.

When children live with their parents, the commandment requires them to obey and respect them. The *Catechism of the Catholic Church* teaches:

> As long as a child lives at home with his parents, the child should obey his parents in all that they ask of him when it is for his good or that of the family. "Children, obey your parents in everything, for this pleases the Lord." (*CCC*, 2217, quoting Col 3:20)

The Fourth Commandment is not just a one-sided relationship requiring obedience and respect from children for their parents. Parents must also honor their children as precious images of God. They must educate their children intellectually and in the social skills. They must provide a safe, warm environment of care, love, forgiveness, tenderness, and service for their children. Moreover, parents have the serious duty to educate their children religiously and morally. Most of all, parents are expected to lead their children to Jesus Christ.

Catholics also see the family as the *domestic church* that mirrors the love and community of the Triune God—Father, Son, and Holy Spirit. In this basic Christian community, we practice the theological and other virtues, hear God's Word, and learn how to pray.

FAQs about the Fourth Commandment

1. What does it mean to *honor* one's parents?

To honor one's parents means to be grateful to them for the gift of life and to respect and obey them because of their roles in the family. As children grow up, the ways they honor their parents change. Young children need to do as they are told and accept the limits parents establish because in so doing they acquire the self-discipline they will need to exercise throughout life. Adolescents need to accept their parents' authority and communicate with parents about their lives and the issues they face. Trusting parents to offer good advice and adhering to the realistic boundaries they set is important at this age because a lot of heartbreak can be avoided and a lot of good accomplished by avoiding temptations that teens typically face. After children leave their parents' home and live on their own, they become emancipated, meaning that they are independent adults. Even as independent adults, however, sons and daughters need to honor their parents, showing them signs of respect and affection and taking their opinions into consideration. When parents become elderly and infirm, children honor them by giving "them material and moral support in old age and in times of illness, loneliness, or distress" (*CCC*, 2218). In so doing, sons and daughters express their gratitude.

2. If parents are negligent and do not meet their obligations to their children, must children still obey and honor their parents?

"If a child is convinced in conscience that it would be morally wrong to obey a particular order, he must not do so" (*CCC*, 2217). Each person's first priority must be to obey God's commandments and not sin by going against the natural moral law written in each person's heart. Therefore, if a parent were to tell a child to do something that was morally wrong, in that situation the child should not obey the parent.

No person is perfect; everyone is a sinner. It follows that parents, too, come up short, and their sons and daughters are likely to be aware of some of their parents' failings. In respect to the Fourth Commandment, "each and every one should be generous and tireless in forgiving one another for offenses, quarrels, injustices, and neglect. Mutual affection suggests this and the charity of Christ demands it" (*CCC*, 2227).

In cases wherein parents abuse their children or are extremely neglectful in meeting their responsibilities, sons and daughters show a great deal of maturity when they forgive their mothers and fathers. The best outcome of such situations is when individuals who have suffered from the absence, neglect, or misconduct of a parent decide not to repeat the behaviors and, instead, to act appropriately when they are blessed with children.

3. What is the purpose of family life?

The family is instituted by God and, "for the common good of its members and of society, the family necessarily has manifold responsibilities, rights, and duties" (*CCC*, 2203). The responsibilities of parents include caring for their children and providing a good example; children have a duty to respect and obey their parents. All members of the family have a right to practice their religion with the expectation that this right will be respected by civil authorities. The Church teaches that God is the Author of creation and that, in marriage, through procreation and the education of their children, parents participate in God's work. The family possesses great dignity because, by God's design, it is "the original cell of social life. It is the natural society in which husband and wife are called to give themselves in love and in the gift of life. Authority, stability, and a life of relationships within the family constitute the foundations for freedom, security, and fraternity within society. The family is the community in which, from childhood, one can learn moral values, begin to honor God, and make good use of freedom."

4. Why should children be born within the covenant of marriage?

When a man and woman get married, they pledge to love and honor each other and to be open to the procreation of new life. The pledge they make and the physical union they achieve constitute the covenant of marriage; their covenant is the profound bond that binds them to one another. By agreeing to marry, they begin a new community, one which will grow as they welcome children into their family. "Marriage and family are ordered to the good of the spouses, to the procreation and the education of children" (*CCC*, 2249). People who are not married have children, but their engaging in sex apart from marriage does not respect the design of the Creator. Children should be born into a stable family, and within this family, they should learn about God's love and plans for them.

5. Why is the family the basic unit of society?

The family is the basic unit of society because the stability and order of the family constitute the "foundations for freedom, security, and fraternity within society" (*CCC*, 2207). Many of the lessons children need to learn in order to live happy and productive lives are learned in the family, and include moral values and the responsibility to reach out to assist those in need.

Because of the importance of the family, other social bodies, such as the Church and the government, should extend support and assistance to families that are in need because of economic hardship or other reasons. The importance of the family for the life and well-being of society entails a particular responsibility for society to support and strengthen marriage and the family. Outside agencies, however, should also respect the prerogatives of parents and should allow families the privacy to which they are entitled.

6. What responsibilities does the political community have in respect to the family?

The political community has a duty to honor the family, to assist it, and to safeguard the freedom of parents to have children and to bring them up within their religious tradition. The family is not just one institution among many; it is the fundamental cell upon which the society is built. Hence, governments should legislate to protect families with the services that enable the rights of parents to own their home, to engage in work to provide for themselves and their children, and "the right to medical care, assistance for the aged, and family benefits" (*CCC*, 2211). The government should also help to protect families from dangers like drug use and pornography, which can damage the lives of individuals and society.

7. Why is the family called a "domestic church"?

The family is called the "domestic church" because it mirrors the love and community of the Blessed Trinity. In the family, we practice the theological and other virtues, hear God's Word, and learn how to pray. Parents are the first heralds of faith to their children. They are to foster in each child a vocation that is suited to him or her and devote special care to fostering religious vocations.

8. What religious priority should parents communicate to their children?

As important as the bonds that unite parents to each other and to their children, and brothers and sisters to each other, these are not the most important ties. The first attachment of a Christian should be to Jesus and to discipleship. Matthew 10:37 says that "whoever loves father or mother more than me is not worthy of me, and whoever who loves son or daughter more than me is not worthy of me." In recognizing this, family members will realize that each person and each family is part of a larger whole, God's human family, and will put God first in affection and loyalty.

Parents are the most influential catechists for their children. Their participation in the life of the Church (especially in Sunday Eucharist), their willingness to evangelize and serve others, and their practice of daily prayer represent the authenticity of their faith to their children.

9. One of the most important decisions parents make is the choice of where to send their children to school. What does the Fourth Commandment require of them?

Parents are responsible for the education of their children, and they have the right to choose a school that corresponds to their beliefs. This right is fundamental. Therefore, parents need to choose schools that affirm their values, and the government needs to support the right of parents to do so.

10. Are Catholics required to obey the government when it demands actions that are contrary to the moral order?

No, Catholics should not obey civil authorities when what they order is contrary to the moral order. Citizens have duties to the state, but these duties require that the citizen act with justice to build up the human community. Citizens are obliged in conscience not to follow the directives of civil authorities when they are contrary to the demands of the moral order because Christians need to obey God and act according to correct moral principles.

Every society's judgments and conduct reflect a vision of humans and their destiny. The Church describes a role for people that places primacy on God's design for human life and that instructs its members to obey just and moral laws. Just as individuals have freedom to act in accordance with God's plan, so, too, does government. Freedom does not mean that individuals or governments can do whatever they feel like doing; freedom means that human persons and human institutions are able to understand what the morally right course is and that they have the ability to choose to follow the right course. It is necessary to do what is morally right, and it is wrong to choose the wrong course or policy. We have freedom to choose rightly. We distort the meaning of freedom to think that freedom allows us to choose to do moral evil. If our government, through its laws, directions, or policies, instructed us to do something that was morally wrong, we should not obey the law, follow the direction, or support the policy.

CASE STUDY:
Honor to Parents after Divorce

M elinda's mom and dad divorced two years ago. Melinda is four-teen years old and has two younger siblings; Matt is eight, and Stacy is six. Her parents share custody, so she and her siblings live with their mom in the house they grew up in Monday through Thursday, and with their father on weekends.

Several weeks ago, it became obvious to Melinda that her dad is now living with his girlfriend Sandy. Sandy is at the apartment when the children arrive on Friday, and she sleeps in the same bedroom as Melinda's dad. Her dad has not said anything about the status of his relationship with Sandy, but he has told his children that he expects them to be accepting and friendly toward her.

Melinda's mom is bitter about the divorce, and she frequently speaks harshly about her ex-husband. Melinda knows that her mother would become very angry if she knew about Sandy, and she thinks that her mom might use the relationship between Sandy and her dad to go to court and request sole custody.

Melinda loves her mother and father and, though she knows it is wrong for her dad to live with Sandy, she wants to try to get along with her as well. She does not think it wise to discuss the relationship between her dad and Sandy with her siblings because they are naïve and probably not even aware of what is going on. She believes that she should honor her father and her mother, but she is confused and depressed as she tries to figure out how to put this commandment into practice. Melinda prays regularly, and she hopes that God will give her the wisdom to know what to do.

EVALUATION

1. What should Melinda's father do to keep his children from being scandalized by his live-in relationship with Sandy?
2. How do you think Melinda's mom could act to facilitate a more harmonious family life despite the divorce?

3. Melinda is confused and depressed, and she prays for guidance. What else, if anything, should she do?

4. Given the situation that she is in, are there things that Melinda could do that would dishonor her mom or her dad, or lead to the further deterioration of her family? What are those things?

CASE STUDY:
Choosing a High School

T ara is an only child. She was adopted, and she is in seventh grade at a rural public school. She gets good grades, is active in student government, and plays softball. There are no Catholic grade schools in the area, and all the children in the region go to the same public school.

Tara's parents are serious about their Catholic faith and have raised Tara in a loving Christian home. The family attends Mass together every Sunday, and they pray together before meals and at bedtime. Also, ever since Tara was a preschooler, her mom and dad have encouraged her to read Bible stories, pray the rosary, and practice other special devotions. Tara accepts her Catholic identity and the religious practices that go with it, and she feels that she is blessed to live in a good and peaceful home.

The bishop in the diocese where the family lives decided that the diocese should have a Catholic high school, and he began a successful fund-raising campaign to build the school. The new school will be a few miles from Tara's home, and bus transportation will be available. The school will open when Tara is in eighth grade, and it will add one grade a year until it can function as a four-year high school.

Tara's parents tell Tara that they have decided that she will attend the new Catholic high school. They have been to meetings about it, and they know that it will offer a solid academic education, extra curricular activities, and, most important of all, instruction in the faith as well as retreats and other opportunities to develop spiritually.

Tara knows she should be happy about her parents' decision, but she feels conflicted. She thinks that the choice of where to go to high school should be hers, not theirs. And, since she has lots of friends where she is and she is doing well, she does not understand why she should have to change school systems. When she tells her parents about her dislike of their plan, they tell her that she needs to get over her reluctance because the decision is final. They also tell Tara that someday she will thank them.

EVALUATION

1. Who do you think should make the decision about where Tara goes to high school?
2. Tara is reluctant to change schools. Is her reluctance justified, or should she have a different attitude? Why?
3. How might Tara benefit by going to a Catholic high school instead of the public school?
4. How would you feel if your parents required you to do something and said, "Someday you will thank us"?

CASE STUDY:
Negligence in Child Rearing

F red and Marge have six children ranging in age from three to sixteen. They live in a row house in a city. Fred has been out of work for the past several months, and Marge has never worked. Neighbors are concerned about the family because the children do not seem to be going to school, there are a lot of arguments with loud shouting at all hours of the day and night, and sometimes the parents appear intoxicated.

Three neighbors meet to discuss the situation. They voice alarm because the disturbances seem to be more frequent and violent and because there does not seem to be any reason to expect things to improve. They brainstorm about what to do. Some of the ideas that surface are that one of them could approach an older child and inquire about how things are going, or that all three of them could ring the doorbell and ask to speak to one or both of the parents. In either case, they would be respectful and ask what they could do to help.

The other ideas are that a neighbor could call the pastor and ask him to visit the family. The family is Catholic, but the neighbors do not know whether or not the pastor is acquainted with them. Alternatively, one of the neighbors could call the office for child and adolescent services and ask that an investigation take place.

The interested neighbors want to help the family and honor the family's privacy and rights. They do not want to bring harm or unnecessary scrutiny to these people. But they are also concerned about the welfare of the children and the competence of the parents to carry out their responsibilities.

EVALUATION

1. For what reasons might this particular family be in distress? What kinds of personal, social, and economic problems affect families?

2. What problems are evident in this case, and what bigger problems may arise?
3. The neighbors consider a number of options to respond to the problems that exist. Which option do you think they should choose, and why?
4. What responsibilities do members of communities, churches, and government have to assist families in distress? How are troubled families helped in your community?

5TH COMMANDMENT

You shall not kill.

Synopsis

The Fifth Commandment forbids murder, the killing of an innocent person. No one has the right to directly destroy any human being. Life is a creative action of God.

The Fifth Commandment is about respecting life. Human life is sacred and should be respected from the moment of conception until natural death.

Christ elevated the Fifth Commandment by forbidding the interior sins of anger and envy that lead to murder and by commanding his followers to love their enemies. Anger should not be expressed in violence. People should reject violence and learn how to live peacefully with each other. The horrors of war and the viciousness of attacks against innocent people in the workplace, schools, or places of public accommodation are crimes that horrify Christian people and all those of good will.

While this commandment does absolutely forbid both murderous thoughts and deeds, reflection on it should lead to an awareness of what a beautiful gift from God life is. At the moment of conception, the life of a new person begins and now, with ultrasound, parents can view pictures of their child months before they hold the baby in their arms. A miracle happens in the womb as the child develops and, after birth, the miracle continues as the infant goes through the various stages of development. Before long the little one will begin to grasp how much love and beauty are offered to her, and, as she grows, it is God's will that she develop feelings of gratitude for the good things of life. This sentiment of gratitude, when joined to respect for life, will lead to sound values and good moral decisions, the total opposite of the irreverence and anger that lead to murder and the other sins against the Fifth Commandment.

FAQs about the Fifth Commandment

1. Why is every human life sacred?

Human life is a gift from God, the Creator of all. Each human being from the moment of conception to natural death is a child of God, and his or her destiny is to be united forever with God. Because God alone is the Lord of life, "no one can under any circumstance claim for himself the right directly to destroy an innocent human being" (CCC, 2258).

2. Why is murder forbidden by divine law?

Murder is forbidden by divine law because "the deliberate murder of an innocent person is gravely contrary to the dignity of the human being, to the golden rule, and to the holiness of the Creator. The law forbidding it is universally valid: it obliges each and everyone, always and everywhere" (CCC, 2261). Murder is an action that reveals the worst possible sentiments: hatred, vengeance, acceptance of violence, and disrespect for God's dominion and the well-being of neighbor and the human community. In the Sermon on the Mount, Jesus told his followers to reject these motivations and replace them with a willingness to turn the other cheek and love one's enemies.

"Infanticide, fratricide, parricide (murder of a parent), and the murder of a spouse are especially grave crimes by reason of the natural bonds they break. Concern for eugenics or public health cannot justify any murder, even if commanded by public authority" (*CCC*, 2268).

3. If someone kills another in self-defense, does he violate the Fifth Commandment?

Taking human life is a terrible thing to do. However, in some circumstances, for some reasons, it is morally acceptable. The *Catechism* states that "the prohibition of murder does not abrogate the right to render an unjust aggressor unable to inflict harm. Legitimate defense is a grave duty for whoever is responsible for the lives of others or the common good" (*CCC*, 2321). When a person is in the extreme situation of having to defend herself against an attacker, she may need to kill him to protect her own life. Police officers sometimes have to kill people who are in the act of killing innocents, or threatening to do so. Soldiers in just wars kill enemy combatants because they are trying to protect the citizens of their country from the danger the enemy poses.

4. Is capital punishment ever justified?

Yes, capital punishment is justified if civil authority determines this is the only way to preserve public order, provide safety for its citizens, and inflict punishment on the criminal. However, the Church understands that such reasons are rarely the only options in today's world. This means that the Church is in reality opposed to capital punishment.

Three factors have caused Catholic leaders to revise their teaching on the death penalty. The first is that non-lethal means are sufficient to defend and protect public safety, so civil authorities should limit itself to such penalties as life in prison without the possibility of parole. Second, by setting such limits, the state would be limiting its punishments to those in conformity to human dignity, because even criminals guilty of heinous crimes are human beings and are entitled to respect. Terminating their lives by executions would manifest disrespect for these lives. Finally, the *Catechism of the Catholic Church* teaches that "by rendering one who has committed an offense incapable of doing harm—without taking away from him the possibility of redeeming himself—the cases in which the execution of the offender is an absolute necessity are very rare, if not practically nonexistent" (*CCC*, 2267). This argument suggests that God's grace and forgiveness are offered to each and every person and that even a criminal guilty of a grave crime could undergo a conversion and possibly become a productive member of society.

5. Do unborn children have the unalienable right to life?

The prophet Jeremiah wrote, "Before I formed you in the womb I knew you, and before you were born I consecrated you" (Jer 1:5). From the moment of conception, when sperm and ovum join to form a unique individual, God, the Creator, establishes a loving relationship with that person-in-becoming. During the process that begins at conception and ends with birth, the fragile new life is innocent and is entitled to protection from his or her parents and from the larger society. The child-to-be has a right to life. Abortion is a serious sin against the Fifth Commandment because it is immoral to kill an innocent. This principle is a fundamental premise of natural law, and it is the responsibility of the Church to affirm its truth.

6. If a pregnant woman has a health crisis such as cancer of the uterus, and treatment for her condition requires removal of the uterus, which would result in her recovery but also the death of the fetus, what course of action should she and her doctors follow?

There are two types of abortions. "Direct abortion, that is to say, abortion willed either as an end or a means, is gravely contrary to the moral law" (*CCC*, 2271). However, the Church also recognizes another classification for abortion, namely *indirect abortion*. An indirect abortion occurs when the unintentional death of the fetus occurs during an absolutely necessary medical procedure such as removal of a cancerous uterus. If medical intervention does not occur, the woman will likely die. A surgeon removes the uterus to eliminate the cancerous organ and save the woman; the fetus dies as a result of the procedure. The abortion is termed indirect because the direct intention of doctor and patient is to save the mother, not to terminate the pregnancy. If the uterus contains a living and nonviable fetus, the fetus will inevitably die, but this result is unintended and hence indirect. There is no direct attack upon the fetus, and its death is regrettably permitted as a secondary effect of an act that needs to be performed and that is morally permissible to perform.

7. What happens to people who procure or support an abortion?

Excommunication is a penalty the Church imposes on individuals who procure an abortion, perform an abortion, counsel a pregnant woman to have an abortion, compel a woman to have an abortion, or pay for an abortion. Excommunication excludes people from taking part in the sacraments, including the Eucharist, and from exercising any Church office of ministry. The penalty of excommunication is only incurred by those listed above if they know beforehand that this will happen if they have or support an abortion. To actually incur the excommunication those in question must know that it is an excommunicable offense at the time that it occurs.

8. Is it morally acceptable for a pregnant woman to undergo amniocentesis or other forms of prenatal diagnosis?

The embryo and fetus are developing persons, and whatever medical procedures are undertaken should be for their care and healing. Therefore, the Church objects to prenatal testing that is done "with the thought of possibly inducing an abortion, depending on the results" (*CCC*, 2274).

9. How is the human embryo to be treated?

The human embryo is human life at the very first moments of its existence. To use human embryos for stem cell research is immoral because these embryos are unique human lives, at their most vulnerable stage. Science is justified to use procedures that respect human life and are in service to human life. Embryonic stem cell research destroys human life and, hence, cannot be morally justified.

10. What is *euthanasia?*

Euthanasia is causing the death of a sick or dying person by taking an action to end the person's life. Intentional euthanasia, whatever its forms or motives, is murder. It is gravely contrary to the dignity of the human person and to the respect due to God. People who think that they are doing a compassionate deed by ending the life of a handicapped, sick, or dying person are mistaken in their judgment. The act remains one of murder and is forbidden by the Fifth Commandment.

11. What medical means does the Church require to sustain a person's life?

Given the sophistication of contemporary medical treatments, it is important to understand that it is often acceptable to discontinue medical procedures, or not begin them, when a person is at the end of life. The *Catechism* states that "discontinuing medical procedures that are burdensome, dangerous, extraordinary, or disproportionate to the expected outcome can be legitimate; it is the refusal of 'over-zealous' treatment. Here one does not will to cause death; one's inability to impede it is merely accepted" (*CCC*, 2278). Having this guidance will not make it easy to reach decisions for loved ones at the end of life because each situation is unique. Therefore, it is advisable for people to share their values with one another and to write down their decisions in an Advance Directive. At the time terminally ill patients or their loved ones are considering medical alternatives, they will need to consult with physicians and may also want to check with their pastors before reaching a final decision.

In regard to the provision of pain medication to people at the end of life, the Catholic Church teaches that "the use of painkillers to alleviate the sufferings of the dying, even at the risk of shortening their days, can be morally in conformity with human dignity" (*CCC*, 2279). The reason for allowing sufficient pain medication is that doctors, nurses, and loved ones are focused on keeping the dying person comfortable and administer the medication for this reason. They do not give the pain medication to kill the person; if they did so with this intention, it would be a morally wrong action.

12. Are people who commit suicide guilty of sin?

Suicide is defined as the willful taking of one's own life and is a grievous sin against the Fifth Commandment. We are required to love God with our whole heart, and our neighbor as our self. Life is a gift from God, and humans are stewards, not owners, of their life. By suicide people contradict the natural inclination to preserve and per-petuate their lives; therefore, suicide is gravely contrary to love of self. People who take their lives disregard their responsibility to love their neighbor because they break their ties with parents, siblings, relatives, friends, colleagues, and the whole human community.

The Church understands that grave psychological disturbances and extraordinary situations like being held in inhumane confine-ment can diminish a person's responsibility for taking his or her life. And the response of the Church after a suicide, regardless of its circumstances, is to pray for those who do this and trust that God is merciful to them.

13. After death, how should the body of the deceased be treated? Are organ donations permissible?

Those who survive are responsible for treating the remains of the dead with respect. The bodies of the dead can be subjected to autopsies for legal or scientific reasons, and the retrieval of organs from the deceased is considered a good practice provided that the deceased person or a loved one gives permission for organ donation. The bodies of the dead should be buried or cremated. The Church permits cremation, provided that the ashes remain together and receive a proper burial.

14. Is it permissible for a living person to donate an organ?

Living persons may donate an organ, such as a kidney, or part of an organ, such as a liver, to a recipient. By so doing, the donor will weaken his body and may undergo psychological stress, but his gift of life to another is justifiable "if the risks incurred by the donor are proportionate to the good sought for the recipient" (*CCC*, 2296). Organ donation is morally right only if the donor acts freely and the procedure does not result in his death. Thus, no living person could donate *both* his kidneys, for this would cause death.

15. How are we obliged to care for our bodies?

Life and health are gifts of God that should be respected. By exer-cising the virtue of *temperance* we need to avoid excess in the use of alcohol and food. Using narcotics for non-medicinal purposes is always wrong. Smoking tobacco is also harmful to health and, therefore, should be avoided. While affirming the obligation under the Fifth Commandment for people to take care of their health, the *Catechism* cautions against succumbing to the cult of the body, according to which people sacrifice everything for the sake of physical perfection and success at sports. By its selective preference of the strong over the weak, such a mentality can lead to the perversion of human relationships.

16. Conditions of poverty and famine lead to premature death. What moral responsibilities do people have to address these conditions?

Concern for the health of its citizens requires that governments help in the attainment of living conditions that allow all people to grow and reach maturity: food and clothing, housing, health care, basic education, employment, and social assistance should be provided. Catholics, motivated by a positive reading of the Fifth Commandment, recognize a moral obligation in charity to contribute to relieve the needs of people who suffer as a result of poverty and famine. In justice, we recognize a moral obligation to address and correct systemic causes of human suffering.

17. Why are anger, vengeance, and hatred considered sins against the Fifth Commandment?

Anger, vengeance, hatred, and intolerance are opposed to peace of heart and goodwill towards others. Anger gives rise to thoughts of revenge and may reach the point of causing an angry person to want to kill or seriously injure someone. If anger is not resisted and proceeds to such a terrible state, it would constitute a mortal sin.

Hatred also leads to behaviors contrary to the requirement to love one's neighbor. Wishing harm to another person and not trying to forgive the other are manifestations of hatred that diminish the person who harbors these feelings.

People who do wrong should be punished by the proper authorities for their wrongdoing and encouraged to become rehabilitated. It would be wrong for an individual to desire vengeance in order to do evil to someone against whom she has a legitimate grievance.

It is appropriate to respect the functions of civil authorities, and it would be wrong for an individual to appropriate those functions to himself or herself.

18. What is scandal, and why is it forbidden?

Scandal is a sinful attitude or behavior that leads another to do evil. The person who gives scandal tempts someone else to do evil. Jesus said, "Whoever causes one of these little ones who believe in me to sin, it would be better for him to have a great millstone fastened round his neck and drowned in the depth of the sea" (Mt 18:6). Jesus' words constitute a warning to everyone, especially those in authority, to lead by good example and not give scandal to others.

19. How is the culpability of killing in war determined?

An individual may take up arms in order to protect his or her fellow citizens from attack. The soldier trains to kill so that the aggressor can be turned back; this is done out of concern for the well-being of innocent citizens and not out of hatred or a desire to kill enemy combatants. Members of the military who kill combatants who have attacked their country are not judged guilty of misconduct. In killing the enemy, they are doing their job, albeit a very difficult one.

20. Are Catholics required to participate in a war effort?

No one, Catholic or non-Catholic, is obliged to participate in killing in war if his conscience tells him all killing is morally wrong. People who reason this way are known as conscientious objectors or pacifists, and governments do not require that they bear arms. According to tradition, in wartime, those of draft age are "obliged to serve the human community in some other way" (CCC, 2311), and this means that conscientious objectors should accept noncombatant assignments.

21. What guidelines must a nation's leaders take into account before deciding to go to war?

Civil leaders should be committed to peace and should not consider war an acceptable way to resolve difficulties with aggressors. They should do all in their power to avoid war and armed conflict. However, if a nation is attacked or is in danger of being attacked, leaders should evaluate the decision to take up arms by considering the following points, known as the "just war criteria":

- the damage inflicted by the aggressor on the nation or community of nations must be lasting, grave, and certain;
- all other means of putting an end to it must have been shown to be impractical or ineffective;
- there must be serious prospects of success;
- the use of arms must not produce evils and disorders graver than the evil to be eliminated. (see CCC, 2309)

22. Why are kidnapping, hostage taking, torture, and terrorism connected with the Fifth Commandment?

Kidnapping and hostage taking cause terror to those who are deprived of their freedom as well as to the human community. These deeds are morally wrong. It is also morally wrong to torture a human being because torturous deeds are an affront to human dignity. Terrorism threatens, wounds, and kills indiscriminately, placing civilians in peril, and it is a grave sin against the Fifth Commandment.

23. What does the Fifth Commandment say about military escalation?

Military escalation does not ensure peace. Far from eliminating the causes of war, it risks aggravating them. Spending enormous sums to produce ever new types of weapons impedes efforts to aid needy populations. The leaders of nations have a duty to protect the common good of all the nations of the world by taking steps to reverse the arms race and to prevent sales of arms to terrorist groups.

CASE STUDY:
War

T hree soldiers are on duty at a checkpoint in a city south of Kabul, Afghanistan. An ambulance approaches and fails to slow down. For one mile before, the checkpoint signs have been placed on the road in Arabic and English, telling all drivers to slow down. The signs make no exceptions for emergency vehicles. Hand signals by the soldiers have been ignored. One of the soldiers has fired warning shots, another soldier, seated in an armored tank, is taking aim at the windshield of the ambulance. The third soldier, standing at the checkpoint, holds a rifle that is also aimed at the ambulance. The rules of engagement under which the soldiers are currently operating direct them to fire on any vehicle that does not stop at the checkpoint. The reason for this policy is that vehicles containing bombs have gotten through checkpoints and have then been parked close to markets and other commercial and residential areas. Given the speed at which the ambulance is traveling, the soldiers have only seconds to react.

EVALUATION

1. How does this case study involve the Fifth Commandment?
2. Since the soldiers are operating under orders to fire on *any* vehicle that does not stop at the checkpoint, should they dispense with deliberating about what to do and just follow orders?
3. What would you do if you were drafted into the military and faced with the probability of being deployed into battle? Explain the justification for your decision.

CASE STUDY:
Abortion

C indy is seventeen. She went to a party with a few girlfriends and got very drunk. The party was at the home of an acquaintance whose parents were away for the weekend. There were thirty or forty people there, both guys and girls. Cindy woke up in an upstairs bedroom. She was naked, and there was blood on the sheets. She did not remember going to the bedroom, and she did not know what happened while she was there. She checked with a friend of hers, Diane, who was also at the party. Diane says she remembers seeing Cindy with a guy early in the evening, but she, too, became too drunk to remember who he was or what happened next.

Two months later, Cindy was feeling rotten. She was throwing up, and she had missed two periods. She used a home pregnancy kit, and it confirmed what she suspected. She was pregnant.

Cindy called Diane and asked to meet her at a local coffee shop. Cindy told Diane about the predicament she was in. Diane listened as Cindy said that her parents "would kill me" if they found out; that she had no idea who she had sex with; and that, should the pregnancy continue, she would get expelled from school because she was on both academic and disciplinary probation. Cindy asked Diane to come with her to the Planned Parenthood agency where she would arrange for an abortion. Cindy wanted to have an abortion and get on with her life. She did not want anyone to know, except Diane, and she begged Diane to keep her secret.

EVALUATION

1. Name some of the violations of the Fifth Commandment suggested by this case study.
2. As Cindy's friend, what should Diane do when asked to accompany her for the abortion? In what ways has and could Diane violate the Fifth Commandment?

3. What are some moral options Cindy has once she realizes that she is pregnant? How would these options be difficult but rewarding?

4. Cindy is afraid of how her parents would react to her pregnancy. Do you think she is being realistic when she claims that they "would kill me" if they found out? What are some typical ways parents would react to such a situation?

CASE STUDY:
Killing an Unjust Aggressor

An armed gunman has taken a position in a tower, which serves as a local landmark. The tower is in the center of town, and from its vantage point, the gunman can see pedestrians on many streets and avenues in the area. There is a lot of pedestrian traffic because there are retail stores, restaurants, businesses, and municipal offices in the area. It is the middle of the day; the weather is clear and dry, and there is nothing to impede the gunman's vision.

Many people have called 911 in the past five minutes to report hearing shots and seeing a man with a gun in the tower. So far, no one has been shot, and there is no way to determine whether or not the man intends to kill and/or wound pedestrians.

The police response team consists of the six members of the force currently on duty. A lieutenant is in charge, and she needs to discuss how the team should react to the gunman in the tower. Her first thought is to have a sniper take aim at him and shoot to kill. Her second idea is to clear the area of pedestrians and open negotiations with the gunman so as to give him a chance to surrender. In the meantime, the man's wife has contacted the police. She says that her husband recently lost his job and that his mother had died only two days before. She also tells the police that they are the parents of two small children.

EVALUATION

1. What is the man in the tower guilty of?
2. What reasons might motivate the police lieutenant to order a sniper to kill the gunman?
3. What reasons would motivate the lieutenant to negotiate with the gunman? How does knowing more about the man's background impact the choices that might be made?
4. What would you do if, in this situation, you were a police officer charged with safeguarding the public?
5. What guidance does the Fifth Commandment offer?

6TH COMMANDMENT

You shall not commit adultery.

Synopsis

The Sixth Commandment forbids having sexual relations outside of marriage. This commandment teaches several positive points about lifelong, committed marriage. First, it is the will of God that married people live out their commitment by being faithful to each other, attentive to each other's needs, and concerned for each other's well-being. Second, spouses should be generous and unselfish as they welcome children as God's gift. Third, love for God, for each other, and for their children should characterize their home, a haven where each, individually, and all, together, seek to grow in wisdom and grace.

The Sixth Commandment teaches the basic principle that God intended sexual intercourse, and all actions leading up to it, to be shared exclusively by a man and woman in the union of marriage.

Through the intimate acts of sexual activity, a husband and wife give themselves totally and exclusively to each other. This act of total self-giving represents their relationship. In marriage, they have committed themselves to each other with no conditions in an exclusive covenant of love. They celebrate their commitment through the gift of sexual sharing in which two people—a man and a woman—become one. This celebration brings pleasure and joy, two gifts God bestows on couples who use the sexual faculty according to God's plan.

Catholics believe that the marriage covenant is lifelong, faithful, and holy. Through it, the couple mirrors Christ's love for his people, which is also permanent, unconditional, and loyal. Thus, marriage is a sacrament, a powerful sign of love that brings a couple closer to Christ and to each other.

FAQs about the Sixth Commandment

1. How does the Church understand the love between spouses?

God created man and woman in his image, desiring that they should love and bond with each other in an intimate union. It is the will of God that humans love each other and that sexual love be expressed in the context of marriage. The Book of Genesis supports this: "God created man in his own image . . . male and female he created them" (Gn 1:27). And, "God blessed them, saying to them: 'Be fruitful and multiply'"(Gn 1:28).

In the encyclical *Deus Caritas Est,* Pope Benedict XVI explained that one of the ways humans love is called *eros*, the "love between man and woman which is neither planned nor willed, but somehow imposes itself upon human beings." *Eros,* in the best sense of its meaning, is the sexual drive, to receive and give love to one's spouse, with all the erotic and emotional feelings that accompany this drive. Pope Benedict described *eros* as good, as part of God's design, but he also teaches that erotic love needs to be complemented by another form of love, *agape*, or self-giving love, which "seeks the happiness of the other, is concerned more and more with the beloved, bestows itself and wants to 'be there for' the other." *Eros* and *agape*, when present in a marriage, express the will of God and fulfill the sexual needs of men and women.

This description of love elucidates a stark contrast to the notion of sex as a recreational activity with a partner whose needs and interests may be of little moment. Human love that embodies elements of *eros* and *agape* requires a commitment between a man and a woman and the recognition that this commitment honors the plan of God in his work of creation.

2. What is *concupiscence*?

Concupiscence is an inclination toward evil caused by Original Sin. More specifically, it refers to the sexual desires and passions that propel individuals to engage in sexual actions without commitment to their partners or clear-headed awareness of consequences. Pope John Paul II said that the way to deal with concupiscence is to become proficient in the practice of the virtue of continence. Continence is an aspect of the virtue of temperance, and the practice of continence enables men and women to dominate, control, and direct drives of a sexual nature.

3. How does sexuality affect a person's identity?

Sexuality affects all aspects of the human person in the unity of body and soul. The body, in its physical and spiritual aspects, with its male or female sexual characteristics, is God's good creation, and it is in and through the body that people communicate love to each other. Each human person, man or woman, should acknowledge and accept his or her sexual identity and understand that the physical sexual differences with which God has blessed humans are designed to be expressed in marriage and family life. Since both woman and man were created in God's image and likeness, they are of equal dignity. By becoming one flesh in marriage, the two sexes give themselves to each other and open their union to the possibility of bringing forth new life. In so doing, married spouses share in God's work of creation. The union of marriage carries such a sacred meaning that Jesus requires respect and support for those who are married, "What God has joined together, no human must separate" (Mt 19:6).

4. How does a person live a chaste life?

Chastity means that a person lives in accordance with the sexual requirements that are part of his or her state of life. For married persons chastity means being sexually active only with his or her partner and being respectful of the partner's needs or desires. For unmarried persons, chastity means refraining from sexual intercourse until marriage. For priests and religious sisters and brothers, chastity means refraining from sexual activity in order to serve God totally.

People in contemporary society have grown accepting of engaged couples living together before marriage. With regard to the engaged, the *Catechism of the Catholic Church* teaches that those who are engaged to marry are called to live in continence. They should see their engagement as a time for building mutual respect and an apprenticeship in fidelity. They should reserve for marriage the sexual expressions of affection that belong to married love (see *CCC,* 2350).

5. Why is lust forbidden by the Sixth Commandment?

God designed marriage as the context for sexual pleasure, with the intention that married spouses alone ought to experience this pleasure. Lust is disordered desire for sexual pleasure, and this pleasure is sought apart from the life-giving and unitive purposes of sexual intercourse that are realized in marriage.

6. Why is masturbation forbidden by the Sixth Commandment?

Masturbation entails the deliberate stimulation of the genital organs in order to derive sexual pleasure; it is a disordered action because it is contrary to the purpose for which sexuality was created, that is, the total giving of one spouse to the other in marriage. The moral responsibility of young people who engage in masturbation may be diminished if this action results from "affective immaturity, force of acquired habit, conditions of anxiety or other psychological or social factors" (*CCC,* 2352).

7. Why is fornication forbidden by the Sixth Commandment?

Fornication is the name for premarital sex. "It is gravely contrary to the dignity of persons and human sexuality which is naturally ordered to the good of spouses and the generation and education of children" (*CCC,* 2353).

8. Why is pornography forbidden by the Sixth Commandment?

Pornography, defined as the removal of real or simulated sexual acts from the intimacy of the partners in order to display them deliberately to third parties, offends against chastity because it perverts the sexual act, the intimate giving of spouses to each other. Pornography does grave injury to the dignity of those who participate in it (actors, vendors, and the public), since each one becomes an object of base pleasure and illicit profit. It immerses all who are involved in the illusion of a fantasy world. Pornography is a grave offense. Civil authorities should respond to pornography by preventing the production and distribution of pornographic materials.

9. Why is prostitution forbidden by the Sixth Commandment?

Prostitution injures the dignity of the person who engages in it, reducing him or her to an object of sexual pleasure. In the practice of prostitution one party pays another for sexual acts in order to experience sexual pleasure. The party who receives payment is often a woman, but can also be a man, a child, or an adolescent. The one who pays for prostitution violates chastity by defiling his or her body. Prostitution is a social scourge that weakens the human community. Society is responsible to address the underlying causes of prostitution as well as the illegal actions of those who pay for sex.

10. Why is rape forbidden by the Sixth Commandment?

Rape is a forcible sexual act performed on an unwilling person. Rape is a violation of justice and charity. Rape is both a crime and a sin. Survivors of rape can suffer psychological trauma for their whole lives. There is never a justification for rape, and it is always to be evaluated as a morally evil action. When a parent or other relative rapes a child, the act is called *incest*, and this is a doubly horrible crime because not only is the victim violated but, also, the familial ties are destroyed. When adults or others in positions of responsibility (e.g., teachers, coaches, priests) are guilty of raping children, the harms to the victim are horrific and the undermining of the social bonds of trust are devastating.

11. Why are homosexual acts forbidden by the Sixth Commandment?

Homosexual acts are forbidden because they are contrary to natural law and they cannot generate new life. Men and women complement, or complete, each other, becoming "one flesh." For homosexuals, this is not possible.

12. Why are some people attracted to members of the same sex?

This is a difficult question, and there is no clear explanation for it. The Church teaches that homosexual persons should accept their orientation and bear the burdens of living chastely because this is the will of God.

13. Why are same-sex unions and civil partnerships prohibited by the Church?

The Church is opposed to same-sex unions and civil partnerships. In 2003, the bishops of the United States stated four reasons for the Church's opposition:

- First, the Church opposes civil partnerships and gay marriages because only a union of male and female can express the sexual complementarity willed by God for marriage. Part of what is necessary for a marriage is the anatomical physiological structure of man and woman, who can unite into one flesh to accomplish procreation. This would be impossible for same-sex partners.
- Second, it is important for society to preserve marriage as the exclusive union of a man and a woman because marriage is the foundation of the family, and respect for marriage contributes to society because it models the way in which women and men live interdependently. The marital union also provides the best conditions for raising children.
- Third, it is not unjust to deny legal status to same-sex unions because marriage and same-sex unions are essentially different realities. In fact, justice requires that society not recognize same-sex unions.

- Fourth, in regard to enacting legislation to provide benefits such as health insurance, pension, and social security to same sex-couples, the bishops state, "It would be wrong to redefine marriage for the sake of providing benefits to those who cannot rightfully enter into marriage."

14. Does the Sixth Commandment condemn homosexuals?

The Sixth Commandment does not condemn homosexuals. Homosexuals are human persons created in the image and likeness of God and are called to live chaste and virtuous lives and to contribute to the common good of society. While it may be hard for homosexuals to abstain from sex, the Church contends that it is possible with God's grace. Sometimes there is discrimination against homosexuals, and there can be wanton violence. The Church teaches that every sign of unjust discrimination should be avoided, and it is totally opposed to violence directed against gays.

15. Why does the Church prohibit artificial contraception?

In marriage, the physical intimacy of the spouses becomes a sign and pledge of spiritual communion. Marriage bonds between baptized persons are sanctified by the Sacrament of Matrimony. The love of spouses for each other comes with a promise of being faithful until death; the acts of intercourse in which they engage are deeply personal and spiritual as well as biological. When people marry, they do so to become united and to bring new life into being from their shared love. The Church teaches that these two goods of marriage, the union of the spouses and procreation, cannot be separated without altering the couple's spiritual life and compromising the goods of marriage and the future of the family. The Church opposes artificial contraception because it reasons that God designed the physical act of intercourse for the purpose of procreation and, if humans contravene that purpose, they act contrary to God's will.

16. What is Natural Family Planning (NFP)?

The Church does not tell couples how many children to have, and it recognizes that there may be circumstances that will keep couples from having children. If spouses, for good reason, do not want to get pregnant, the Church teaches that they can engage in marital intimacy during the naturally infertile times in a woman's cycle, or after child-bearing years, without violating the meaning of marital intercourse in any way. In learning the woman's fertile and infertile times, and using this knowledge to avoid pregnancy, the couple is cooperating with the body as God designed it.

Natural Family Planning differs from contraception because natural family planning respects God's gift of complete sexual intimacy and contraception does not. The United States Catholic Bishops explain:

> When couples use contraception, either physical or chemical, they suppress their fertility, asserting that they alone have ultimate control over this power to create a new human life. With NFP, spouses respect God's design for life and love. They may choose to refrain from sexual union during the woman's fertile time, doing nothing to destroy the love-giving meaning that is present. This is the difference between choosing to falsify the full marital language of the body and choosing at certain times not to speak that language. (*Married Love and the Gift of Life*)

17. Why is adultery a sin against the Sixth Commandment?

Adultery is marital infidelity, that is, sex between two partners at least one of whom is married to another party. Adultery constitutes a grave injustice against one's spouse because it violates the covenant on which a marriage is based. The stability of the marriage union is threatened by adultery, as well as the welfare of children. Jesus condemned even adultery of desire, saying, "You have heard that it was said, 'You shall not commit adultery.' But I say to you, everyone who looks at a woman with lust has already committed adultery with her in his heart" (Mt 5:27–28).

18. Why is divorce a sin against the Sixth Commandment?

When spouses marry, they pledge their love and fidelity until death. The union they establish is meant to be a permanent one for their well-being and the well-being of their children. Divorce breaks the contract to which the spouses freely agreed. There can be situations in which irreconcilable differences prompt spouses to separate and live apart. Depending on the reasons for a separation, it can be morally acceptable. It should be noted that in some divorces only one party is guilty of undermining the marriage. In this regard, the Church teaches:

> It can happen that one of the spouses is the innocent victim of a divorce decreed by civil law; this spouse therefore has not contravened the moral law. There is a considerable difference between a spouse who has sincerely tried to be faithful to the sacrament of marriage and is unjustly abandoned, and one who through his own grave fault destroys a canonically valid marriage. (*CCC*, 2386)

19. Why are polygamy and free union sins against the Sixth Commandment?

Polygamy means being married to more than one spouse and usually refers to a man having more than one wife. Polygamy is not in accord with the moral law because it denies the equal dignity of one man and one woman on which marriage is based. In order to conform itself to God's design, the love for one's spouse must be total and exclusive, and polygamy makes this impossible.

In a so-called *free union*, a man and a woman refuse to go through a marriage ceremony and instead choose to live together in an arrangement involving sexual intimacy. By so doing, they reject the dignity of marriage and the requirement that they publicly pledge their love and fidelity. The Church teaches that trial marriages or living together for a time to discern compatibility before making the commitment of marriage is immoral. The reasons are that the sexual act must always take place within marriage; people need to truly commit to each other, and casual arrangements allow them to split up when problems arise; and only a free, total gift of one person to another in marriage can become the basis for a lifelong bond.

CASE STUDY:
Internet Pornography

Ron and Rick are fourteen-year-old twins. They were always very close, playing together, hanging out, and confiding in each other. Over the past six months, things have changed, and Rick is concerned. When he asks Ron to do something or wants to talk, Ron always has an excuse why he can't. Ron used to enjoy being outside and playing basketball, but lately he seems to always be in the house staring at his computer.

Ron and Rick each have their own laptop. One day, Rick left his laptop in his locker at school, and he used his brother's to check on something. Rick knows that he should not have done so, but he also checked Ron's web browsing history. What he discovered alarmed and scared him. Ron had been online with several pornographic websites and had been chatting on some of them. The reason Ron was not around and Rick had access to his computer was because Ron had left school that day and gone downtown on what he said was an "errand." Rick wondered if Ron's errand had anything to do with the chat rooms he had been visiting.

Rick was confused as to what he should do next. His parents would be home soon; Ron had said he would be home after dinner. Rick did not want his relationship with his brother to further deteriorate, but he also did not want his brother to make a decision that he would really regret.

EVALUATION

1. Was Rick justified to look at Ron's computer? Are there any situations when a person should have the right to complete privacy?
2. How could viewing pornography negatively affect Ron?
3. Now that Rick knows what Ron has been doing, what should Rick do?

4. Ron went into town on an errand. Given his Internet activity, what suspicions do you have about the trouble he could get into on this errand?
5. If the twins' parents find out what is going on, what actions should they take?

CASE STUDY:
Birth Control

S usan and Brian have been dating for eight months. They are high school juniors, and they get along very well. They have very strong sexual feelings for each other, but they have not engaged in intercourse. Last week they almost lost control but managed to stop in time. Brian tells Susan that he loves her and that he knows how strongly she feels about him. He says that they should not cause frustration to each other by denying the pleasure of sex. He asks her if she is willing to use birth control.

Susan says that he should get condoms and that she is willing to have sex if they use protection. Brian says that they have to be extra sure she will not get pregnant, so she should get birth control pills and take them, too. This way, if a condom tears or something, they can be sure to prevent a pregnancy.

Susan asks Brian if he will stand by her and the baby if, even with her taking birth control pills and his using a condom, she gets pregnant. Brian answers that by being careful they will eliminate the chances of a pregnancy and that neither of them should have to think about having a child. They both have plans to go to college and start careers.

Susan feels sad because Brian did not answer her question and reassure her of his love and sense of responsibility. She does not know how to express her feelings to Brian, and so she says only that she needs to think about this and that they will need to talk some more before she is able to make up her mind.

EVALUATION

1. Brian and Susan feel sexually attracted to each other. Should this attraction dictate the actions they take, or are there other considerations they need to bear in mind?
2. Are there any foolproof methods for preventing pregnancy? What are these methods?

3. Why do you think Brian did not reassure Susan that he would stand by her and their child if she were to become pregnant?

4. Susan is trying to resolve a dilemma. What insights should she derive about whether or not to have premarital sex from Catholic teaching related to the Sixth Commandment?

CASE STUDY:
Adultery

Emily and Jake have been married for twenty-six years, and they have three children, one in high school, one away at college, and one living on her own. Their marriage has not been a very happy one because of many problems that they have had to deal with. Jake lost two good jobs, and, for the past eight years, he has been under-employed in a warehouse working the night shift. Emily has always worked part-time to supplement the family income; for the past ten years, she has suffered from a debilitating nervous condition that drains her of energy and leaves her depressed. When she is home from work, Emily is generally napping or watching TV. She shows Jake little attention and leaves most of the housework for him to do.

Emily and Jake's children are high achievers, and both their adult daughter and son in college financed their educations by obtaining scholarships and summer jobs. The high school junior is on the same track, so, fortunately, college expenses are not a concern of this couple.

Emily's depression and lethargy have been getting to Jake. He has begun to feel depressed, too, and has become increasingly dis-satisfied with his marriage. There is a new night-shift manager at the warehouse, an attractive divorcee a few years younger than Jake, and she has been acting friendly toward him, talking to him at break time and sharing jokes and anecdotes. His manager makes him feel alive and happy, and he begins to fantasize about having a relationship with her. Jake suppresses the feelings of guilt he also experiences and tells himself that God doesn't want him to be unhappy and that maybe he should pursue something more with his manager.

EVALUATION

1. What problems do Emily and Jake confront in their marriage? Are these typical or exceptional problems?

2. What responsibility does Emily bear to improve their relationship? What responsibility does Jake bear to improve their relationship?

3. When they married, what promises did they make to each other? Do Emily and Jake's present circumstances relieve them of their vows made at marriage to love and be faithful to one another?

4. When Jake feels attracted to his supervisor and fantasizes about her, what should he do?

5. In spite of their older ages, how would Emily and Jake's children be affected by adultery, separation, or divorce?

7TH COMMANDMENT

You shall not steal.

Synopsis

The Seventh Commandment outlaws theft, that is, taking someone else's property against his or her will. The Seventh Commandment rests on the foundation of justice. Justice requires that God's gifts of food, clothing, and shelter are meant for each of God's children and that it is wrong for one person to have an abundance while another lacks what is needed to live in accordance with human dignity. Further, the Seventh Commandment rejects lifestyles centered on greed and exploitation, and it advocates the practice of charity by which believers share with those in need. The quest for greed will lead us away from the true goal of human life. Instead, this commandment points out that the way to be happy is to be content with having what we need and being committed to helping those in need to better themselves.

The Seventh Commandment is also the foundation for Catholic social teaching. Catholic social teaching consists in the witness of the Catholic Church to action on behalf of justice for all people. The basic premise of Catholic social teaching is that it is important for morally good people to be concerned about and active in building just societies that are stable and prosperous and that promote human rights. The conviction underlying this teaching is that God has entrusted the planet earth and the politics and culture of society to human persons and that God requires that people be committed to justice.

Catholic social teaching consists of hundreds of documents that have been developed in response to ethical issues confronting the human community. As a contemporary example, people throughout the world are considering how to respond to scientific data related to climate change, and the Catholic Church is examining how its unique perspective and teachings might be helpful in addressing this issue.

Catholic social teaching has roots in Scripture. For example, the prophets of the Old Testament reminded the Hebrew people that they were in a special relationship to God, that he had made a covenant with them, and that he expected his people to act with justice toward everyone, especially the disadvantaged. Words of the prophets to extend care to the widow, the orphan, the immigrant, and the hired hand still motivate religious people to respond to the needs of the disadvantaged.

The New Testament records many instances of Jesus' outreach to the poor and outcasts. Jesus provided the insight that each and every person has innate dignity and is entitled to respect. By his warmth toward the blind, lepers, an adulteress, a Samaritan woman, and tax collectors, Jesus taught that there is but one human family and each member deserves a seat at the table. The second stipulation of the Great Commandment states, "You shall love your neighbor as yourself" (Mt 22:39). From Jesus himself, therefore, we learn that religion is not just between the believer and God. The believer is also required to love his neighbor. And who is one's neighbor? In the parable of the Good Samaritan, Jesus teaches his followers that Christians should act as neighbor to anyone who is in need.

The Seventh Commandment is most associated with respect for the property rights of others. If people do not follow this common sense dictate, then it would be very difficult for a society to function. But there are many other ways to abuse a person's rights in this regard. Here are some examples of violations against the Seventh Commandment:

- deliberately keeping objects that someone lends to you

- keeping things you find without making an effort to locate the rightful owners
- business fraud
- paying unjust wages
- price-fixing
- participation in corrupt systems that often leads to some unfair financial, political, or professional gain or advantage
- the taking for personal use of supplies or common property that belongs to an employer or larger enterprise
- tax evasion
- doing shoddy or poor quality work, or failing to complete work that's been paid for
- check or invoice forgery
- expense-account padding in order to make unfair, personal financial profit
- wasting time or materials
- willfully damaging public or private property

FAQs about the Seventh Commandment

1. What constitutes theft, and what should be done to make reparation for theft?

Theft is taking something that does not belong to you; not returning something that was borrowed; not trying to find the owner of something that was lost, and, instead, keeping the item; defrauding people of wages; and failing to pay what is owed, such as tuition or taxes. Individuals who are guilty of theft need to make restitution, that is, to pay back what they wrongfully took. Debts, such as taxes or payments of bills, also need to be met, as do late payment penalties.

2. How should justice be practiced in the administration of material possessions?

Justice is a complex virtue that requires temperance on the part of individuals so that people do not become obsessive and greedy in respect to acquiring material possessions and they remain open to the needs of others so as not to do harm to others. Justice takes three forms:

- *Commutative* justice, which obliges strictly; it requires safeguarding property rights, paying debts, and fulfilling obligations freely contracted. Without commutative justice, no other form of justice is possible;
- *Legal* justice, which concerns what the citizen owes in fairness to the community;
- *Distributive* justice, which regulates what the community owes its citizens in proportion to their contributions and needs.

3. How should charity complement justice?

Catholics should serve the poor and try to meet their material and spiritual needs; in so doing they believe that they serve Jesus. In the gospel, we read, "What you did not do for one of these least ones, you did not do for me" (Mt 25:45). But we should not be satisfied with giving food, shelter, and alms because the spirit of the Seventh Commandment requires much more than this.

Catholics should also take active roles in promoting social justice through private and government programs that lead to respect for human dignity and economic opportunities for people all over the world, and especially in poor nations. Christian values support fair trade, an end to the arms race, and the economic development of all countries so that their citizens can live in accordance with their innate human dignity. It is a duty in solidarity and charity for citizens of rich nations to support their governments to make up for the resources they have taken from poor nations that have not been fairly compensated. Obviously, direct aid to poor countries following natural disasters is appropriate, but rich nations also need to participate in reforming international economic and financial institutions so that poor nations can advance economically and their poor citizens, who are mostly peasants, can have a better standard of living.

4. How can sharing the earth's resources be compatible with owning private property?

The Church teaches that owning private property is in accordance with God's will because it is reasonable for individuals to own property so that they can meet their basic needs and the needs of those dependent on them, thus preserving their human dignity. However, prior to asserting their individual right to own private property, people should recognize the fact that God gave the earth to humankind so that people acknowledge that what they own may benefit others as well, and there should be a willingness to share with those in need. Those who own goods of production such as land, factories, practical or artistic skills, are obliged to employ them in ways that will benefit the greatest number. While the Seventh Commandment forbids theft, it should be noted that "there is no theft if consent can be presumed or if refusal is contrary to reason" (*CCC*, 2408), so that in situations of grave immediate need if individuals take food, shelter, or clothing that belongs to someone else, they are not guilty of wrongdoing. This is because the right to own private property is not an absolute right and a legitimate exception to it exists when individuals in extreme distress need to take things in order to survive.

5. How does the Seventh Commandment address the enslavement of human beings?

Each and every human person is created in the image and likeness of God and is of inestimable dignity. Therefore, any act or enterprise that leads to the enslavement of human beings, to their being bought, sold, and exchanged like merchandise, in disregard for their personal dignity, is a sin against the dignity of persons and their fundamental rights. No person should be used as a source of profit for someone else, and human trafficking and enslavement are gravely wrong.

6. How should humans be good stewards of the earth?

God entrusted the stewardship of the earth and its resources to humankind to meet human needs; God directed humans to care for the earth and enjoy its fruits. The goods of the earth are for the whole human race, and for all generations. As stewards, men and women are entrusted with the care of the earth so that they are required to respect all of creation and to act to meet their neighbors' needs as well as their own. It would be morally wrong to exploit or pollute the earth or to hoard the goods of nature.

7. Is it morally permissible for humans to use and kill animals?

Just as humans were created by God, so were animals; as God's creatures, animals deserve to be respected by humans. However, respect for animals does not mean that humans cannot use and kill animals. It is legitimate to use animals for food and clothing because humans rightly exercise dominion over animals. And "medical and scientific experimentation on animals is a morally acceptable practice if it remains within reasonable limits and contributes to caring for or saving human lives" (CCC, 2418). It would be morally wrong, however, to cause animals to suffer or die needlessly or to spend money on them that should be spent to relieve human misery.

8. What is the purpose of work?

Work is a duty that humans have in order to carry on the work of creation and meet human needs. St. Paul wrote: "If anyone was unwilling to work, neither should that one eat" (2 Thes 3:10). Work has positive aspects in that it allows people to use their talents and to build up the human community. Work also has negative aspects in that it may require a lot of effort and entail boredom, frustration, and fatigue. Work is the way people earn the wages they need in order to support their families, pay their bills, assist the needy, and save for the future.

The modern workplace can be a place of competing interests in which the interests of management and those of labor conflict. When conflicts arise, "efforts should be made to reduce these conflicts by negotiation that respects the rights and duties of each social partner: those responsible for business enterprises, representatives of wage-earners (for example, trade unions), and public authorities (*CCC*, 2340). In times of economic crisis, it is especially important to understand the fundamental principles that should be honored regarding work and workplace interaction because these principles should be borne in mind as negotiations are undertaken.

Workers should receive fair pay for their labors. What constitutes fair pay? This question was succinctly answered by the Second Vatican Council: "Remuneration for work should guarantee man the opportunity to provide a dignified livelihood for himself and his family on the material, social, cultural and spiritual level, taking into account the role and the productivity of each, the state of the business, and the common good" (*CCC*, 2434, quoting *Gaudium et Spes*, 67:2).

Because work is so important to the dignity and the practical needs of men and women, unemployment constitutes a major moral and economic issue. Unemployment almost always wounds its victim's dignity and threatens the stability of his or her life. Besides the harm done to individuals personally, it entails many risks for their families as well. This is why all sectors of society are morally obliged to counter unemployment and take action to make jobs available to all who need to work to maintain their economic and human dignity.

9. What connection exists between the Seventh Commandment and international development?

On the international level, inequality of resources and economic capability is such that it creates a gap between nations. On the one hand, there are nations possessing and developing the means of growth and, on the other, nations accumulating debts. It is morally wrong for prosperous nations to prosper at the expense of poor nations; rich nations have a moral responsibility to assist poor nations in their development. Respect for God's plan for creation should motivate political leaders of nations throughout the world to work toward the full development of human society in all nations. Lay people need to participate in social action to bring attention to global issues and work toward resolution of the problems that exist.

CASE STUDY:
Buying Stolen Goods

Tim has been saving money from doing odd jobs to buy a laptop computer with wireless capacity. He wants to have a laptop so that he can take notes in class, surf the web, and do assignments while commuting to and from school. He has been saving for a few months, and he now has close to $400. Tim has been researching laptops, and he has come to the conclusion that the type of computer he wants will cost between $500 and $600.

Tim and his friend Mike go to a mall to have lunch at the food court. As they walk across the parking lot, they pass a van with a man and woman standing outside. The side doors of the van are open and there are a number of items in clear view. The woman asks Tim and Mike if they are in the market for an iPod or a laptop. Tim answers that he wants to buy a laptop but that he has not yet saved enough. The conversation continues, and the woman eventually shows Tim a state-of-the-art laptop in sealed packaging that retails for close to one thousand dollars. It is far superior to the models that Tim has been considering. When he asks how much they are asking for the computer, they reply, "$275." The man asks Tim if he wants it and reminds him that, at that price, it will not last long.

Tim says that he does not have enough money on him to make the purchase and that he needs to think it over. The people tell him that they expect to be in the mall parking lot for a few hours, and they suggest that he go home, get his money, and come back and buy the laptop. They say that he needs to act right away as they will not be there tomorrow.

EVALUATION

1. What do you think about Tim's plan to save money he earns to buy a laptop? Do you think that owning a laptop is necessary for a student? What other technologies (e.g., iPod, Internet phones) are "absolutely" necessary today?

2. Regarding the man and woman in the mall parking lot who are selling merchandise from their van, is there anything about this scenario that makes you suspicious or concerned? Be specific.

3. Tim can get a great laptop for $275. Do you think he should he go through with the purchase? Explain.

4. How does the Seventh Commandment help to answer this case study?

CASE STUDY:
Rights of Illegal Immigrants

Carlos and Jaime came to the United States from Mexico in order to work. Both men have relatives in Florida who they plan to live with. Both men also have wives and children who will remain in Mexico. Most of the money they make will be sent back to Mexico for the support of their families.

In the winter months, Carlos and Jaime work harvesting the citrus crops. Except when it rains, the work is steady and they get paid. The pay does not amount to a great deal, but they are frugal, and it provides enough for them and their loved ones to survive.

When citrus picking ends in the spring, it becomes more difficult for Carlos and Jaime to get work. Their routine changes, and they wait at a designated pick-up point each morning at six. This is where contractors come to pick up day laborers for work in construction and landscaping. Sometimes they get hired for the day; often they do not. There are many other undocumented immigrants who also wait for work, and Carlos and Jaime think themselves fortunate when one morning they are chosen by a contractor who is putting in a swimming pool and who tells them that he will need them for at least two weeks. They agree to work for $12 an hour, and plan to work twelve-hour days, unless it is raining, in which case there will be no work.

At the end of the first week, the men expect to be paid approximately $800. They are unsure whether they will be paid for the time they spent on short breaks or for lunch. When they approach the contractor and ask for the money he owes them, the contractor says that there is a problem with the homeowner and that he has not been paid, so he will also need to hold off on paying them. He asks for their cell phone numbers and tells them that he will call them when he has their money. He also says that the job is now on hold, so he will not need them next week. He tells them that they have been good workers, and he will let them know when work will resume.

EVALUATION

1. Why are Carlos and Jaime working? Do the needs of their families supersede the laws of the United States?
2. Do you think it is right for Carlos and Jaime to work without documents and without paying taxes?
3. Comment on the contractor's failure to pay Carlos and Jaime. What recourse do Carlos and Jaime have?
4. The Seventh Commandment requires commutative justice. What is commutative justice and how does commutative justice apply to this case?

CASE STUDY:
Clear-Cutting a Rain Forest

There is a rain forest in central Brazil that is home to millions of species of animals, birds, flowers, and insects, many of which have not yet been classified. Besides its biodiversity, the rainforest also functions as a giant air filter, removing carbon dioxide from the atmosphere and replacing it with oxygen. The rain forest is approximately five square miles in area and contains an inestimable number of exquisite mahogany trees that could be used to manufacture beautiful furniture.

A speculator buys the property from an elderly widow whose family has owned it for generations. She sells it because she wants to settle her affairs before she dies, and she wants the money to distribute to her heirs and various charities. The widow attaches no conditions to the sale of the property; once it passes to the new owner, it is hers to do with as she chooses.

The speculator negotiates with a furniture company headquartered in the United States. The acreage will be clear-cut; the mahogany will be sold to the furniture manufacturer, and the speculator will make a substantial profit. The furniture manufacturer also projects a profit from the sale of valuable furniture to wealthy clients. Many people will be employed in both clearing the forest and building the furniture, so from the furniture company's perspective, this can be seen as a winning venture all around. In the future, the speculator sees the possibility of selling the land to a developer for a housing development.

EVALUATION

1. What are any moral reasons to object to clear-cutting the rain forest?
2. Do you think that the widow acted appropriately when she sold the rain forest without attaching any conditions to the sale? What conditions might she have incorporated into the contract?

3. Comment on the role of the speculator: should the speculator's role be viewed as positive or negative? Why?

4. Is it morally acceptable for wealthy people to buy fine furniture, or are there reasons why they should not? What reasons occur to you?

5. People will be employed to clear the property and sell and transport the lumber, make the furniture, and sell the furniture. These families will be better off on the basis of this employment. Nevertheless, are there reasons to be negative about this employment? What are the reasons?

6. What directions does the Seventh Commandment offer regarding preserving the environment?

8TH COMMANDMENT

You shall not bear false witness against your neighbor.

Synopsis

The Eighth Commandment declares that it is wrong to tell lies, and it is especially wrong to harm another person's reputation either by lying about the person or by revealing his shortcomings without justification. The positive side of the Eighth Commandment requires that believers respect and live by the truth. This demands moderation and discipline in speech and an unwillingness to lie, exaggerate, or humiliate in order to gain an advantage.

People today tend to be well informed about nutrition, rejecting junk food and opting instead for a healthy diet. It is good that we have become educated about the connection between what we eat and our overall health. In Jesus' time, the religious leaders called Pharisees tended to be obsessed about Jewish dietary laws. In the ancient world, people could get sick, and even die, after eating contaminated meats, seafood, and dairy products. The Pharisees' interests went beyond concern for the health of the community, however, and they made it their business to evaluate their neighbors as worthy or unworthy based on how they complied with the hundreds of regulations that eventually made up Jewish dietary laws.

Jesus repudiated the Pharisees, calling them hypocrites. As we consider the Eighth Commandment, what Jesus said to them is especially instructive for us: "It is not what enters a person's mouth that defiles the person; but what comes out of the mouth is what defiles one" (Mt 15:11). With this comment Jesus teaches us that by such sins as false witness and slander we diminish our moral goodness and undermine our growth in grace. (Jesus did not question the reasonableness of not eating tainted food, and his instructions are not an argument against good nutrition today; instead, Jesus' words point out the truth that by our speech we should express the love of neighbor we nurture in our hearts.)

By our nature, all humans are inclined toward the truth. It is part of our human dignity to seek the truth, especially religious truth, and to follow it once it is discovered. This is the positive meaning of the Eighth Commandment.

FAQs about the Eighth Commandment

1. What does it mean to be truthful and to tell the truth?

People who follow Jesus should live in the truth. This means that they should speak the truth and be sincere in their words, attitudes, and actions. Truth is a virtue, or habit of right living, by which a person shows respect for God's will and also deals with his or her neighbor in a just and upright manner.

2. What is *detraction* and how does it harm others?

Detraction is the sin of speaking about another's faults and failings to persons who do not know of these shortcomings, without a valid reason. Those who engage in gossip are frequently guilty of the sin of detraction.

3. How do perjury and false witness offend against the truth?

When it is made publicly, a statement contrary to the truth takes on a particular gravity. In court, it becomes false witness. When the statement is made under oath, it is perjury. Perjury and false witness may contribute to condemnation of the innocent, or the exoneration of the guilty, and they gravely compromise judicial fairness and justice.

4. Why is it morally wrong to make fun of people?

Belittling or ridiculing others is a wrongful use of speech that causes hurt feelings and denies to others the respect that they deserve. Each individual is entitled to a good reputation and to be spoken of in a respectful manner.

5. What is *calumny* and how can people be guilty of calumny?

Calumny is speaking falsely and negatively about others; calumny harms the reputation of others and provides the basis for reaching false judgments concerning them. Calumny is unjust and wrong.

6. Why is it morally wrong to tell a lie?

When people lie, they speak or act against the truth in order to lead others into error. Lying undermines one's relationships with others, and lies offend God who wants us to live honestly with each other.

7. Is every lie a serious sin?

It is always wrong to lie, and people need to be truthful. Whether a lie is a venial or a mortal sin is determined by the nature of the untruth that is spoken, along with the circumstances, intentions, and the harms that follow. If there is grave injury to the virtues of justice and charity, a lie may be a mortal sin; in cases of less than grave injury, it would be a venial sin.

8. **How should a person go about deciding whether or not to provide information to someone who is asking for it? Must one always provide truthful information to those who ask for it?**

It may or may not be appropriate to reveal the truth to someone who asks for it. The good and safety of others, respect for privacy, and the common good are sufficient reasons for being silent about what ought not to be known or for making use of a discreet evasion. The duty to avoid scandal often commands strict discretion. No one is bound to reveal the truth to someone who does not have the right to know it. Therefore, if a person asks about an issue that one does not wish to discuss because of valid reasons for keeping silence about the matter, there is no moral requirement to answer the person, and there may even be a moral requirement not to respond. Giving an evasive answer that suggests one does not know or is not certain is justifiable.

9. **What is meant by "professional responsibility" to keep a confidence?**

Professionals, such as physicians, lawyers, and soldiers, are bearers of confidential information, and they must keep this information secret. There may, however, be exceptional cases when keeping the secret is likely to cause very grave harm to the one who confided it, to the one who received it, or to a third party, and in which the very grave harm can be avoided only by divulging the truth. Those who possess such information bear the burden of determining when a case is so exceptional that they must reveal what they hold in secret.

10. **Are priests ever allowed to reveal what is told to them in the Sacrament of Penance?**

The secret of the Sacrament of Penance is sacred, and cannot be violated for any reason. Priests are under an absolute requirement not to repeat anything that is confessed to them. The sacramental seal is considered inviolable; this means that it may never be broken.

Therefore, it is wrong for a confessor in any way to betray a penitent by word or in any other manner or for any reason.

11. What responsibilities do the media have to transmit the truth?

Society has a right to receive truthful information about issues of importance. Nothing can justify recourse to disinformation for manipulating public opinion through the media. In addition, the media should avoid sensationalism, character attacks, and invasions of privacy in its reporting because such tactics weaken the social fabric and distract citizens who seek to be well informed.

12. What responsibilities does art have to witness to the truth?

The *Catechism of the Catholic Church* reminds us that all sacred art, by its nature, is directed toward expressing in some way the infinite beauty of God in works made by human hands. In view of its lofty purpose, artistic expressions, be they musical or visual, should honor the truth and goodness of God and should be created so as to inspire positive sentiments in men and women.

CASE STUDY:
Keeping a Friend's Secret

Sharon and Katie have been close friends since grade school. They are now high school sophomores. Katie began gaining weight in middle school, and she ignored her eating habits for a few years. Some classmates made remarks about Katie's weight, but most said nothing about it, at least not so that she could hear them. Sharon never belittled Katie or made her weight an issue and, because of her understanding and loyalty, Katie considers Sharon her best friend.

At the beginning of sophomore year, Katie began to be concerned about her weight and went on a diet. She was very strict with herself, and she managed to get to her goal weight in three months. True to form, Sharon did all the things a friend should do when Katie was dieting. She encouraged her, and she never once suggested that Katie go off the diet and enjoy a high-calorie treat. Sharon felt proud of Katie and happy for her when she lost the extra pounds.

Recently, Sharon has become concerned about Katie because Katie's disposition has changed and because she has been eating junk food items and then vomiting to get rid of them. Sharon asks Katie why she spends so much time in the bathroom and asks, "You're throwing up what you eat. Right?" Katie starts to cry and admits that she has developed a problem with eating and purging (bulimia), and she tells Sharon that this is to be a secret just between the two of them. Katie tells Sharon that she is her friend because Sharon has always been loyal and has never done anything that would hurt Katie.

Sharon is confused. She wants to respect Katie's privacy, but she has heard that bulimia is a serious disorder, and she thinks that Katie may need professional help to stop her self-destructive behavior.

EVALUATION

1. Katie and Sharon are friends and, generally speaking, friends should keep secrets. What are some exceptions to this rule?

2. What should Sharon do in this situation? Should she keep her knowledge about Katie's problem to herself, or should she share this information?

3. If Sharon should tell someone, who should that someone be? Why?

4. Speculate on the reasons Katie is eating and purging, and consider constructive advice that you might give her.

CASE STUDY:
Strategy for Attaining Better Grades

Tim is a popular high school junior with slightly above-average grades. The grades are really Tim's issue; if he could show dramatic improvement over the last three semesters in high school and raise his grade point average from slightly above 3.0 to closer to 3.5, he would have a much better chance of being admitted to a "dream college," not the local community college his parents say that he must attend if he doesn't improve his grades.

Tim is in four of five classes with a fellow junior named Marlene. She is hardly a social person; in fact, her shyness, plain dress, and some quirky behaviors have made her a bit of an outcast since way back in elementary school. Tim has been in school with Marlene for all of his school career, yet he can't remember even speaking with her.

Marlene, for all of her uniqueness, is in line to be the class valedictorian. Tim decides befriending Marlene can only help him improve his chances for understanding the course material and perhaps obtaining some secrets she can pass on for getting better grades. Tim asks Marlene if she will study with him, and she agrees. The two begin to spend a lot of time with each other in the library, at lunch hour, and even after school at each other's homes. Tim is surprised to discover that he has grown to really like Marlene and appreciate her for who she is.

It didn't take Tim's friends, both males and females, long to ask what was going on between the two. Tim considers the reputation he has cultivated among his friends and classmates and feels like saying something like, "Oh, I know she's weird. I'm just using her to improve my grades." But he thinks about how that would hurt Marlene and how he really doesn't believe that anyway. Now some of his friends are teasing Tim and telling others that Marlene is Tim's girlfriend.

EVALUATION

1. What do you think of the importance Tim has attached to attending his "dream college"?
2. Is there anything wrong with Tim's motivation for seeking out Marlene for help? Explain.
3. How should Tim answer those who question his reasons for hanging around with Marlene?
4. What else could Tim do for Marlene to help others appreciate her the way that he does?
5. How does this case study connect with the Eighth Commandment?

CASE STUDY:
A Neighbor's Question

Laura's neighbor is a retired elderly gentleman who has a lot of time on his hands and who is both lonely and inquisitive. Laura's parents have discussed Mr. Burton's situation at the dinner table and have said that they think the kind thing to do is to stop and chat because he lives alone and has few visitors. In fact, Laura's family makes talking to Mr. Burton one of the acts of kindness to which they commit themselves.

Laura's sister Cindy is nineteen years old, and she is seven months pregnant. Cindy got pregnant during the fall of her freshman year at college. She told her parents right away, and they agreed with her to keep the pregnancy secret because Cindy has decided to surrender her baby for adoption. Cindy wore loose fitting clothes at school and did not tell her classmates about her condition. Laura knows about Cindy's pregnancy, and she is totally supportive of her sister.

When spring semester ended, Cindy went to stay with an aunt who lives in a different state. She will give birth there and surrender the baby. Cindy plans to rejoin her family at the end of July and spend the rest of the summer at home.

One day in late May, Laura meets Mr. Burton, and he presses her about where Cindy is. He says that she should be home from college by now, and he misses seeing her. "Where is she? What is she up to?" he asks Laura. Laura is a truthful person, but she is deeply discomfited by her neighbor's prying questions.

EVALUATION

1. Should Laura give an honest answer to Mr. Burton's question and disclose her sister's pregnancy to him? Why or why not?
2. If Laura decides not to answer Mr. Burton's questions with the truth about Cindy's pregnancy, how should she handle the questions?

3. Cindy does not want people to know about her pregnancy. Nowadays people are generally open about such pregnancies. Do you think that she should likewise be open?

9TH COMMANDMENT

You shall not covet your neighbor's wife.

Synopsis

Covet means "to desire something that is not one's own." This commandment directly refers to the covenant of marriage. But it is also concerned with purity of heart and the struggle for moderation. Modesty "protects the intimate center of the person" and guides us as to how we look at others and behave toward them in conformity with their dignity and our solidarity with them. Recall from the teachings about the Sixth Commandment that there are sexual actions that are unacceptable for Christians. The focus of the Ninth Commandment is also on sexual behavior, but this commandment concentrates more on one's thoughts and ideas, rather than one's actions. Of course, it is thoughts and ideas that give rise to actions, so the two are interrelated.

Jesus said that humans should love themselves. One of the ways the Ninth Commandment teaches us to love ourselves is to cultivate sentiments of contentment about our lives. After people marry, they need to develop attitudes of love and appreciation for their spouse and reject temptations to disparage the spouse and fantasize about others. Infidelity in thought leads to infidelity in action, and, ultimately, leads to pain and suffering for all those who are affected.

FAQs about the Ninth Commandment

1. Humans are composed of mind, body, and spirit. How are these components supposed to work together?

God created humans in God's image and endowed them with a special dignity that results in their being superior to animals and all other forms of creation. Their gifts of intellect and the power to choose from among alternatives enable humans to become good persons. As they ponder the special characteristics that they possess as humans, men and women recognize that besides their bodies, they also have spiritual aspects, that is, the ability to think, choose, love, and pray. Understanding that humans possess these spiritual aspects leads them to acknowledge the power and importance of their spiritual dimension. Becoming a good person entails making good choices in all aspects of one's life, including the sexual sphere. However, it is not always easy to follow through and behave chastely, and many people acknowledge that they experience a certain tension; "a certain struggle of tendencies between 'spirit' and 'flesh.'" They want to practice the purity of heart that the Ninth Commandment requires, but they experience temptations that make it difficult to achieve their goal. The mind and the spirit, as vital aspects of the human person, are meant to direct the desires of the flesh so that the whole person—mind, body, and spirit—conforms his conduct to God's will.

2. How does the Ninth Commandment address concupiscence?

Recall from the discussion on the Sixth Commandment that concupiscence can refer to any intense form of human desire. St. Paul identifies concupiscence with the rebellion of the "flesh" against the "spirit," that is, with experiencing sexual desires that people know they should not act on. Concupiscence unsettles and disturbs people; without being in itself an offense, it inclines people to commit sexual sins.

Pope John Paul II taught that people need to learn how to master concupiscence of the flesh. The pope explained that concupiscence refers to the sexual desires and passions that propel individuals to engage in sexual actions without commitment to their partners or clear-headed awareness of consequences. Concupiscence is an aspect of human nature that the Church teaches is an outgrowth of Original Sin and that needs to be acknowledged and guarded against. Pope John Paul II said that the way to deal with concupiscence is to learn about and become proficient in the practice of the virtue of continence. Continence is an aspect of the virtue of temperance and the practice of continence enables men and women to dominate, control, and direct drives of a sexual nature.

It is often accepted today both in popular media and actual practice that it is not realistic to expect men and women who are not married to abstain from sex. The Catholic Church disagrees with this argument and maintains that it must speak the truth about God's design in creation, about God's intentions regarding human love, and about the benefits to human persons who live by God's plan. And, the Church insists, with God's grace and help, it is possible to practice continence.

3. Why does the Ninth Commandment say that one "shall not covet your neighbor's *wife*"?

As usually written the Ninth Commandment states, "You shall not covet your neighbor's wife." The reason the commandment says "wife" is because of its ancient origins; at that time women were considered subservient to their husbands, even their husband's property, and men were warned not to desire sexual pleasure with a woman who was married. In modern times, the Ninth Commandment is understood to forbid nurturing a desire for sexual intimacy with another person's spouse, either the husband or the wife.

4. Why are marriage vows sacred?

Marriage vows are sacred because marriage is the foundation for human society. Married people establish their own homes, and they bring children into the world and raise their children, caring for them and for each other. Not only are the vows by which spouses commit to each other sacred, the family life that springs from marriage is also sacred. Therefore, everyone should respect the commitment spouses make to each other when they marry, and should support married people through good times and bad. It would be a grave sin to look upon a married person with sexual desire, and temptations of this kind need to be rejected.

5. What does this passage from Matthew 5:28 mean: "Everyone who looks at a woman with lust has already committed adultery with her in his heart"?

Lust is having a craving for sexual pleasure with a person who is married to someone else or someone not in a committed relationship to the person experiencing the craving. It is natural for men and women who are married to desire sexual pleasure with each other, and there is no sin in such feelings. Likewise, it is natural for engaged people to feel strong sexual cravings for each other, although they need to wait until they marry to follow through on their feelings.

By indulging a powerful feeling of sexual attraction for someone to whom one is not married or engaged, an individual would sin because thought precedes action and it is dangerous to allow one's thoughts to focus on what is immoral.

6. How are our bodies "temples of the Holy Spirit"?

It is an awesome truth that the Holy Spirit is with each baptized person, and it leads to respect for oneself and one's neighbor. This respect rightly affirms that each human body, one's own and one's neighbor's, is "a manifestation of divine beauty" (CCC, 2519) and leads to respect for others, rather than encouraging lustful impulses toward them.

7. What is meant by purifying one's heart and practicing temperance?

It is from the mind or the heart that evil thoughts come; illicit sexual desires come from the heart. In the Beatitudes, Jesus said: "Blessed are the clean of heart, for they will see God" (Mt 5:8). "Clean of heart" refers to people who have trained their minds and their wills to do what God requires of them and to restrain illicit sexual impulses. According to the Catechism of the Catholic Church:

Purity of heart is the precondition of the vision of God. Even now it enables us to see according to God, to accept others as "neighbors"; it lets us perceive the human body—ours and our neighbor's—as a temple of the Holy Spirit, a manifestation of divine beauty. (*CCC*, 2519)

8. What types of spiritual practices should people engage in so as to work toward having purity of heart?

A person can work toward having purity of heart by getting in the habit of trying to discern and follow God's will in all of life's choices. Especially in regard to ideas and images that are sexually provocative, the individual should try to discipline feelings and imagination so as to avoid temptations that would lead to sin. It is also important to practice prayer because it is through God's help that people practice continence.

9. What is modesty? How do societies set standards for modest behavior?

Temperance is a virtue that requires that people avoid extremes in behavior and that they choose reasonable ways of acting. Modesty is an aspect of temperance. People need to be modest, that is, they need to refuse to unveil what should remain hidden. Accordingly, people clothe their bodies appropriately and refrain from seeking sexual gratification by looking at pornographic images. Respect for oneself and others demands as much.

In practicing modesty, people need to object to images that exploit the human body as well as any attempts to denigrate the body. While ideas about modesty vary from culture to culture, in all cultures there is an awareness of the spiritual dignity of the human person and the protections that should be put in place to preserve this dignity. Moral permissiveness, which is widespread in contemporary Western society, "rests on an erroneous conception of human freedom" (*CCC*, 2526); and people need to acknowledge the truth that this permissiveness is contrary to the moral law.

10. What role does pornography play in undermining purity of heart and modesty?

Pornography exists in many forms: in photos, videos, online, and in print. The aim of pornography is to tempt viewers to think or act in impure ways. Use of pornography for sexual stimulation is morally wrong because individuals are supposed to engage in sex so as to express their bond of love with their spouse. Pornography undermines this worthy goal. In addition, by its definition, pornography is the opposite of modesty because, with modesty, people clothe and respect themselves and acknowledge their responsibilities to God and each other. In pornographic media people are intentionally or unintentionally degraded, and their dignity is denied.

11. How should sexuality be approached in a positive way?

In his encyclical *Deus Caritas Est*, Pope Benedict XVI said:

> The love-story between God and man consists in the very fact that this communion of will increases in a communion of thought and sentiment, and thus our will and God's will increasingly coincide: God's will is no longer for me an alien will, something imposed on me from without by the commandments, but it is now my own will, based on the realization that God is in fact more deeply present to me than I am to myself. Then self-abandonment to God increases and God becomes our joy. (17)

With these words, the pope explains that sexuality and love should be approached in a positive way. Acknowledging the wisdom of God who created us male and female and establishing boundaries for humans to observe in their thoughts and actions serve as guidelines that encourage us to be happy, holy, and fulfilled.

CASE STUDY:
Choosing Entertainment

our young women—Tina, Monica, Sara, and Allison—share a hotel room during a class trip to a ski resort. They are in their second year of high school, and they return to their room after a day on the slopes and a late dinner, followed by a sing-along. Although it is after 10:00 p.m., none of the girls feel tired and ready for bed.

They have prepaid for the room and all payments for the trip have been handled by their chaperones, who are also their teachers. They were told that if there were any further charges to the hotel bills because of phone calls made from the room or any other costs incurred, they would be responsible for payment.

Tina suggests that they play cards until they are ready to settle down. Monica has a different idea; she wants to watch an adult movie. She has checked out the room's television service, and one of the channels shows adult films. There is a cost, and she says that she has enough money with her to pay for it. No one will know until after they have seen the film and, if there are any complaints, they can tell their chaperones that they didn't know about the kind of content adult movies contain. Monica says she is registered to the room as an eighteen-year-old and that she has the right to watch whatever she chooses.

Sara feels intimidated by Monica's suggestions. Although she is nervous about watching a pornographic movie, she does not want to oppose Monica on the chance that she will be teased by Monica. Allison does not want to watch the movie. She thinks a lot about her personal values and wants to develop into a virtuous young woman. Allison is reluctant to share her aspirations with her roommates, and she feels uncomfortable about the situation she finds herself in. Tina acts oblivious to the situation and acts like she only wants to play cards. She doesn't want to get in trouble. Watching the film is the last thing she feels inclined to do.

EVALUATION

1. What is morally wrong with the choice to watch the pornographic movie?
2. Which of the four young women has the strongest personality and exercises the greatest influence?
3. Which of the young women is thinking correctly and what moral standards does she manifest?
4. How difficult will it be for Sara to oppose Monica? Given the situation Sara is in, how could she oppose Monica? Why?
5. What religious motivation could Tina and Allison summon to reject Monica's plan? How should they communicate their thinking to Monica and Sara?

CASE STUDY:
Selecting a Swimsuit

Audrey goes shopping with her mom. Summer is just around the corner, and Audrey needs a few things, including a swimsuit. In the past year, Audrey's body has matured, and she has become a very attractive young lady.

Audrey knows that she could attract a lot of attention if she chooses a swimsuit that reveals a lot of her body in the style made popular by swimsuit models that are featured in an annual sports magazine. On the other hand, she thinks it is sad that the society views the models as objects and seems to only be interested in one part or another of their anatomies. Even if the models make a lot of money for being photographed in swimsuits, they lose some of their dignity in the process.

At the store, Audrey picks out two swimsuits that fit her well. One is a one-piece that her mom considers modest and appropriate. The other is a bikini that leaves nothing to the imagination. When she tries on the bikini, Audrey sees herself as she never did before. *If I wear this swimsuit*, she thinks, *girls will be jealous of me and boys won't be able to take their eyes off me.* Audrey's mom cautions Audrey that the bikini is very revealing, but she tells her that Audrey is growing up and that it is time for Audrey to start making her own choices about what she will be wearing.

EVALUATION

1. Audrey is curious about the attention swimsuit models receive. What should she do about this curiosity? Should she encourage it or try to overcome it? Why?

2. What factors are likely to occur to Audrey when she rehearses the advantages she might gain from having the bikini? Are there reasons she should choose the one-piece suit? What are these reasons?

3. Comment on Audrey's mother's role in this episode. Should she have limited Audrey's choice, or is she acting responsibly in telling Audrey that the decision is up to her?
4. How does the Ninth Commandment address this case study?

CASE STUDY:
E-mailing a Co-worker

aughn is a manager at an information technology company. He is married and has two teenage children. He and his wife have a civil relationship; they were closer when they were first married, but in recent years they have grown apart.

A new employee, Cheryl, joins Vaughn's team; she was recently married, and she is very outgoing and attractive. Vaughn finds himself looking at her with sexual interest and daydreaming about spending time alone with Cheryl.

Vaughn knows that there is a company policy against forming romantic relationships with other employees. He also knows that, since Cheryl is married and so is he, he should keep a professional distance between them. As far as he can tell, Cheryl regards him as her manager, nothing more, so that all the feelings are coming from his end.

In spite of his better judgment, Vaughn allows himself to be pre-occupied with thoughts of Cheryl. His infatuation with her takes a toll on him; he has trouble sleeping and is cranky with his wife and children. At work he finds himself distracted and experiences trouble getting his job done.

Vaughn gets to a point where he feels like he needs to do some-thing: either resolve to get his mind off Cheryl or make an advance in order to determine whether he has any chance of getting her to agree to become friendly. He feels weak and compulsive, and he decides to start e-mailing Cheryl; in his e-mails he will mix business-related issues with subtle suggestions that they meet, and then wait to see how she responds.

EVALUATION

1. Vaughn and his wife have been growing apart. Should they be indifferent to the situation, or should they take steps to correct it? What should motivate them? What steps could they take?

2. Cheryl is an attractive married woman, and Vaughn wants to have a relationship with her. What does this tell us about Vaughn?

3. If Cheryl becomes aware that Vaughn is trying to establish a romantic relationship with her, how should she respond?

4. What are some legal and moral issues regarding this situation?

10TH COMMANDMENT

You shall not covet your neighbor's goods.

Synopsis

Similar to the Seventh Commandment, the Tenth Commandment opposes greed, envy, and avarice (the seeking of riches and the power that comes with them). The spirit of this commandment encourages detachment from material things so that we do not crave luxury items. However, the Tenth Commandment does not discourage us from securing the basic necessities we require to sustain ourselves and our dependents. If we do not spend our energies wishing for big ticket items or coveting those material goods our neighbors possess, we will be able to channel our energies into cooperating with God's grace in building up our spiritual lives.

In the Sermon on the Mount, Jesus taught, "For where your treasure is, there also will your heart be" (Mt 6:21). Disordered attachment to goods turns people away from God. Christians keep in check the strong desire to accumulate wealth and envy at the expense of others by practicing acts of love and humility and by being open to God, who is the only one who can fill up our craving hearts.

Jesus teaches that we should desire him first, and his Father's Kingdom, and then he will give us all that we need. He requires a "poverty of spirit" for us, that is, a certain detachment from earthly riches that eventually pass away. The pursuit of goods can enslave us. On the other hand, pursuing the Lord as the source of our true fulfillment makes us both free and happy: "Blessed are the poor in spirit, for theirs is the kingdom of heaven" (Mt 5:3). The antidote to dependence on material things is to choose God's Kingdom and righteousness above all.

FAQs about the Tenth Commandment

1. What does *covet* mean, and how does covetousness detract from being a good Christian?

The message Jesus' followers learn from the New Testament and from the teaching of the Church is to practice simplicity of life and trust in God. Covetousness for material things is contrary to the Tenth Commandment because by being covetous people exceed the limits of reason and covet unjustly what is not theirs or is owed to another. In being covetous, individuals exceed the bounds of reason and develop attachments to things that they don't own, setting their desires and their hearts on having these things. Covetousness is an interior sin that distracts people from pursuing legitimate goals; by indulging covetousness, people gravitate to other sins such as theft.

2. How does envy undermine individuals and the human community?

People should limit their desires for money and material things to having enough to enjoy a modest standard of living. It is appropriate for parents to want to have sufficient income to provide for their material needs and those of their children, to be able to provide their children with a good education, and to save enough to insure a comfortable retirement. These are reasonable financial goals. The sin of envy prompts people to want to have what belongs to others and become jealous of those who have more than they do. "Envy is sadness at the sight of another's goods and the immoderate desire to have them for oneself. Envy is a capital sin" (*CCC*, 2553). Capital sins are so-called because they lead to other sins. In the case of envy, this sin undermines good relations between individuals, and it erodes the common good of communities because people are moved to steal and to defraud their neighbors in order to obtain what is not rightfully theirs.

3. What is meant by *greed* or *avarice?*

Greed, also called *avarice,* is a sin that springs from a disordered desire for riches and power. Avaricious people have been known to go so far as to commit injustice and harm others in order to obtain what they want. Greed is a sin that is manifest in an excessive desire to possess more money and other material things than one needs or deserves. Greed motivates people to steal, to gamble excessively, to act in fraudulent ways, and to even manipulate financial markets in view of a temporary benefit without regard for long-term consequences.

4. What is the purpose of money?

Money is the means of barter used in modern society. People need to have money to buy the things they require to sustain life. The way people meet many of their obligations, or bills, is by paying money to those who provide services. Money can also be given to charities that use the money to assist the needy in a variety of ways. Many people save money for their retirement years so that they will be able to pay their bills, and they will not present a burden to their children or to society. It is not wrong or sinful to approach money in these reasonable ways. However, it would be sinful to nurture a love of money and to obsess over money, always wanting more than one reasonably needs. The simple statement, "He who loves money never has money enough" rings true because it affirms the fact that an emotional and spiritual attachment to money undermines the priority a Christian should place on doing God's will.

5. Is it morally wrong to want to have a good income and enjoy a comfortable lifestyle?

It is not morally wrong to want to have a good income and enjoy a comfortable lifestyle. What Christians need to bear in mind is that they should not set their hearts on material things. Rather, that they should observe the requirements of justice in their relations with others, and they should guard against wanting to have what rightly belongs to others.

6. What virtues should a Christian cultivate in order to be faithful to the spirit of the Tenth Commandment?

The spirit of the Tenth Commandment encourages Christians to practice simplicity and trust in God. Living a simple life implies setting one's priorities by studying the Scriptures and making Jesus' values one's own. Jesus taught by his example. He came to establish the Kingdom of God, and those who follow him are supposed to use their talents to build up God's Kingdom, a world of justice and peace where the needs of all, especially the poor, are met.

Jesus counseled his followers to believe in God's providence and to overcome tendencies to feel anxious about tomorrow. People who trust in divine providence and who commit themselves to living a simple life can look forward to the promise of the beatitude that states, "Blessed are the poor in spirit, for theirs is the kingdom of heaven" (Mt 5:3).

7. What is materialism and how is it manifest in society?

The United States and other first world countries are capitalist nations. The economies of capitalist nations function through production, sales, and purchase of goods and services. These activities of buying, selling, and producing are carried out by the so-called private sector; government can intervene by issuing regulations that limit or restrict these activities. Capitalism, as an economic system, has positive and negative aspects. When capitalism is functioning well, there is prosperity, and people are able to earn wages and obtain the goods and services they need to live decent lives. When a major component of a capitalistic system becomes dysfunctional, such as the banking and financial sectors, much hardship and suffering follow.

Materialism, a moral issue, arises in capitalistic societies. The many consumer goods that are produced are presented to buyers with the alluring suggestion that these goods will bring happiness and joy to their owners. This is a false and seductive promise, and all people should see it for what it is. It would be a grave mistake to think that clothes, vehicles, jewelry, yachts, or mansions could bring happiness to humans. Relentless pursuing of items of this type instead of seeking first the Kingdom of God is against the principle Jesus taught in the Beatitudes.

8. If worldly riches do not satisfy the human heart, what does?

The Scriptures teach us that to see God is to possess God. The *Catechism of the Catholic Church* states: "Whoever sees God has obtained all the goods of which he can conceive" (*CCC*, 2548). The human person is created with an eternal goal, to pass from this life to the next, and to enjoy the beatitude of God for all eternity. In this life people will never be completely satisfied with what they have because complete satisfaction will only be attained in Heaven. People will not be completely happy until they are united with God for eternity. In the meantime, they can achieve joy and satisfaction by following God's way and not being distracted by envy, greed, and materialism.

9. How does following the Tenth Commandment relate to the other commandments in the Decalogue?

The Ninth Commandment points out that it is wrong to desire illicit sexual pleasure. The Tenth Commandment forbids wanting to have the property of others. Desires for things that do not belong to an individual lead the individual to theft and fraud, which are forbidden by the Seventh Commandment. An extreme desire for another's property could result in violence and murder, which are forbidden by the Fifth Commandment. The First Commandment tells us that we should worship God alone; avarice, which is condemned by the Tenth Commandment, entails worshipping material possessions rather than the living God.

CASE STUDY:
A Struggling Family

S teve's parents recently lost their jobs. They both worked at an over-night package-delivery facility, and the business went bankrupt. Most of the other people in the community also worked for the same employer, and they, too, are out of work. There are no other major employers in the area and prospects for finding jobs in the region are bleak. Many of their neighbors who are unemployed have listed their houses for sale. They want to sell their homes and move to other places to find work and begin anew.

Steve's parents tell him what is going on. Steve is fifteen, and they feel he is old enough to understand the family's situation. Steve's four-and seven-year-old siblings are not part of the conversation because his parents think that they would not be able to grasp the reality that confronts them.

His parents tell Steve that the family is now living on unemploy-ment insurance that will run out within a year. After that, there are some savings, but the savings will not last more than six to eight months. They tell Steve that he will need to find part-time jobs like landscaping and snow shoveling to help out. Things will have to change, and they will have to cut back. His parents tell Steve that they are canceling cable TV and Internet service, and that they will not be able to take the family vacation they planned. Also, the family food budget is going to be cut; there will be no expenditures for clothing; the thermostat will be turned down; and he will have to leave the school he is attending and transfer to the local public school because they cannot afford the private school tuition.

Steve is shocked by what he hears. Over the next few days he becomes sad and angry. Why should his life take such a harsh turn? He envies his best friend Mark, whose wealthy grandparents subsidize that family's income. There are no changes in Mark's family's lifestyle. Steve becomes increasingly moody and thinks about running away from home. Anything to avoid looking for work mowing lawns for elderly neighbors.

EVALUATION

1. Comment on how Steve's parents are approaching the family's economic crisis. Can you suggest a different, or better, approach?

2. What makes Steve feel so sad and angry? Does his emotional reaction indicate that he has a spiritual problem?

3. Is it fair that Mark's family is not in economic crisis and Steve's is? What responsibility, if any, does Mark's family have to Steve's family and to others in the community?

4. Steve's parents tell him that he will have to change to a public school, because they can no longer afford to pay tuition. Are there any steps that authorities at private schools can take to assist students like Steve?

CASE STUDY:
Rachel's Lifestyle

Rachel is a Catholic young woman who graduated from college two years ago and landed a very good job at a consulting company. She had immediate success and has been assigned an assistant, but she prefers to do everything herself; in this way she has total control over whatever project she is working on.

Rachel is the first one at the office in the morning and the last one to leave. She complains that she has no time for herself, but she sees no connection between her hours at work and her lack of leisure time.

Rachel wants to keep advancing in her career, so she is always working on a second project, even without her manager's knowledge. This way, when her current project is finished, she will be a step ahead on the next project. Her commitment to her projects forces Rachel to work during lunch, skip breaks, and avoid conversations with her co-workers. She becomes angry when things do not move along as quickly as she wants them to and, on weekends, she feels guilty because she is not working.

Rachel's thoughts are mostly about the future and how far she will get professionally if she keeps performing above expectations. She wants to buy a condo in a prestigious building and fill the closets with designer clothes. She wants to buy a fancy car to park in the garage. Growing up, Rachel always wanted an affluent lifestyle similar to what some of her classmates enjoyed; her family lived modestly, and her parents were far from well-off. She is determined to do whatever it takes to become affluent.

Rachel is super organized at work, but she forgets family birthdays and finds reasons to miss family gatherings. She is glad that she is on her own because there is no one telling her that it's Sunday and that Mass is at ten o'clock.

EVALUATION

1. Consider Rachel's attitudes toward work and her behaviors. Do you see any problems in her approach to her job? Describe these problems.

2. What values does Rachel manifest? Are Rachel's values consistent with those suggested by adherence to the Tenth Commandment?

3. Rachel wants a high-end condominium, a closet full of designer clothes, and an expensive car. What are some reasons people seek out these things? Will these possessions make her happy? Why, or why not?

4. Rachel avoids her family and does not go to Mass. What advice would you offer her in regard to the decisions she has made regarding family and the practice of religion?

CASE STUDY:
Gambling

Brian believes that average people who work for a living will never be rich, and he wants to be rich so that he can have all the things that money can buy. Brian will graduate from high school in a few months. His family is neither well-off nor poor; his dad works, his mom stays at home and keeps busy with five children. Brian is the oldest. Brian has always been given what he needed in terms of clothes, fees for school, and a modest allowance. But for the past year or so, Brian has become increasingly critical of his parents' approach to life. They believe in working hard, providing for their family, saving money, and following the teachings of the Catholic Church. Brian thinks that this approach to life is boring and that it has made his parents embrace a life of drudgery. He wants to enjoy life and not get bogged down in monotony.

Brian is fascinated with gambling: horse racing, playing cards for money, and casino games. He considers himself very smart and believes that if he studies gambling techniques, he will become a successful gambler and reap financial gains in the process. He knows that he is cool and detached, and he considers his temperament an asset that perfectly complements his ambition. He has already won $3,330 in one sitting of online poker, though he did lose all but $200 of his winnings in a later game.

By not landing a boring job and getting tied down with a wife and children, Brian believes he will be free to make money at his own time and in his own way. Gambling, to him, seems much more exciting and interesting than the nine-to-five job that occupies his father day in and day out. And, best of all, when the rewards flow in, Brian will be able to buy the flashy car and other things that he has come to crave.

EVALUATION

1. What sinful impulses impel Brian?
2. Why do you think Brian is critical of his parents' values?

3. Brian thinks that his father's job is boring and constitutes drudgery. Is this a fair assessment?

4. The Tenth Commandment does not outlaw gambling or games of chance, but it does judge them as morally evil when they enslave a person or keep a breadwinner from supporting a family. If you were advising Brian about what to do after he graduates, of what would your advice consist?

APPENDIX:

OTHER SOURCES OF CATHOLIC MORALITY

Two Great Commandments

According to both Sacred Scripture and Sacred Tradition, the heart of the moral life consists in love of God, self, and neighbor. Jesus himself answered this way when he was asked, "Which commandment in the law is the greatest?" He said:

> You shall love the Lord, your God, with all your heart, with all your soul, and with all your mind. This is the greatest and the first commandment. The second is like it: You shall love your neighbor as yourself. The whole law and prophets depend on these two commandments. (Mt 22:37–40)

When we love God, ourselves, and our neighbor, we fulfill the law, and we do what God wants. Jesus told us that God loves us and desires our undivided love and devotion in return. Jesus taught that by properly loving ourselves, taking care of our health, and not allowing our minds to become preoccupied with greedy, lustful, or angry desires, we follow God's plans for humanity. Finally, Jesus taught us to be generous and forgiving toward others, to desire their well-being, and to live in peace with them so as to build his Kingdom on earth. Jealousy, false speech, sex outside marriage, and disrespect for parents or for children are all among the behaviors that are contrary to love and that erode the human community. Love of neighbor fulfills the law of God, and those who love their neighbors do not violate the second part of the Decalogue.

The Beatitudes

Jesus was a great teacher. His most memorable lesson is from the Sermon on the Mount. In this teaching, Jesus surprised his listeners by making promises to them that sustain hope in the midst of tribulations and urging them to view the tribulations of life from a different perspective. These so-called Beatitudes, from a word meaning "supreme happiness" are:

> Blessed are the poor in spirit, for theirs is the kingdom of heaven.
>
> Blessed are they who mourn, for they will be comforted.
>
> Blessed are the meek, for they will inherit the earth.
>
> Blessed are those who hunger and thirst for righteousness, for they will be satisfied.
>
> Blessed are the merciful, for they will be shown mercy.
>
> Blessed are the clean in heart, for they will see God.
>
> Blessed are the peacemakers, for they will be called children of God.
>
> Blessed are those who are persecuted for the sake of righteousness, for theirs is the kingdom of heaven.
>
> Blessed are you when they insult you and persecute you and utter every kind of evil against you [falsely] because of me.
>
> Rejoice and be glad, for your reward will be great in heaven. (Mt 5:3–12)

Everyone wants to be happy and to have a good life. God put this desire in the human heart. Since the goal of the Christian is the beatitude of Heaven, the way we approach the use of earthly goods needs to be in keeping with the law of God. As we saw when we reviewed the commandments, possessions will not make us happy, stealing will harm us as well as the victims of theft, and lustful desires will hurt us and others. When we work to build up God's Kingdom by seeking to bring justice and peace to all people, we experience a contentment and satisfaction that cannot be found in material goods or selfish ambition. When our lives on earth are complete, we can enjoy the vision of God and we will be fulfilled. Although our happiness can never be whole in this world, we will participate in God's joy and grace to the extent that we accept the limits of the human condition and try to see life, death, suffering, and deprivation with the wisdom that Jesus offers us.

The *Catechism of the Catholic Church* sums up the reason for human existence when it states: "God put us in the world to know, to love, and to serve him, and so to come to paradise. Beatitude makes us 'partakers of the divine nature' and of eternal life" (*CCC*, 1721). The happiness Jesus promises requires that we make moral choices. We need to purify our hearts of bad instincts and seek first the love of God. Jesus teaches that "true happiness is found in God alone, the source of every good and of all love" (*CCC*, 1723).

Precepts of the Church

The Church is a living family not limited by time or space. The Church has leaders in the Magisterium who continually call us to the moral truth of Jesus, who is "the Way, the Truth, and the Life." Like any family, the Church has rules to follow. These are known as the precepts of the Church and must be obeyed by all Catholics. The precepts of the Church are:

1. *You shall attend Mass on Sundays and on holy days of obligation and rest from servile labor.*

   This precept corresponds to the Third Commandment and makes explicit the requirement that Catholics continue the tradition established by the early Church of commemorating Jesus' Resurrection and keeping holy Sunday, the first day of the week.

2. *You shall confess your sins at least once a year.*

   This rule encourages reception of the Sacrament of Penance in which Catholics receive God's forgiveness after they have sinned. The requirement to confess applies to those who are guilty of gravely offending God by committing mortal sins. Whether or not individuals are guilty of mortal sin, the grace of the Sacrament of Penance provides spiritual benefits, and people should receive this sacrament regularly.

3. *You shall receive the Sacrament of the Eucharist at least during the Easter season.*

   This precept requires a minimum amount of participation in the Eucharist during the most sacred season of the year, the season when Catholics commemorate the Passion, Death, and Resurrection of Jesus. It is the Church's desire that Catholics receive the Eucharist much more frequently than once a year. The third precept sets an absolute minimum standard.

4. *You shall observe the days of fasting and abstinence established by the Church.*

   The Church requires that Catholics fast on Ash Wednesday and on the Fridays of Lent. All Catholics are obliged to abstain from meat on those days. On other Fridays throughout the year, Catholics are encouraged to abstain from meat or perform some other act of self-denial or Christian charity. The rationale for mandating fasting and abstinence is to encourage people to master their thoughts and desires and carry through on following such commandments as the Ninth and Tenth. (Fasting requires not eating between meals and allows for eating three meals: breakfast, lunch, and dinner.)

5. *You shall help to provide for the needs of the Church.*

   Catholics have the duty to support the Church with gifts of their time and talents, and with monetary gifts.

Magisterium

The Latin word *magister* means teacher, and the term *magisterium* refers to the teaching authority of the pope and bishops in the Catholic Church. In their teaching and preaching, these pastors of the church explain principles contained in the commandments that need to be followed in order to live a moral Christian life. When moral questions arise, it is the duty of the hierarchy to pronounce on issues that fall within the natural law.

Documents and Encyclicals

A Compendium of the Social Teaching of the Catholic Church, issued in 2004 and available online, contains an overview of the teachings of the Church on the whole range of social issues including justice, human rights, the family, work, economic life, politics, international relations, war and peace, and the environment.

The encyclicals *Evangelium Vitae* (1995) and *Fides et Ratio* (1998) of Pope John Paul II examine issues not covered by the *Compendium. Evangelium Vitae (Gospel of Life)* explains the reasons why life is to be respected from the moment of conception to natural death and, hence, why such practices as abortion, capital punishment, suicide, and euthanasia are against the natural moral law. In this encyclical, Pope John Paul II also addressed the needs of the sick and the dying and the responsibilities of caretakers and loved ones around the bedside.

Fides et Ratio (Faith and Reason) explains the Catholic approach to morality that is based on the natural law, written by God, on the human heart. There is no conflict between faith and reason and, by properly applying the wisdom of God and human reason to moral issues, the leaders of the Catholic Church are blessed with the ability of being able to determine the correct resolution for the most complex moral issues of our times. When they attempt to reach conclusions on moral questions, pastors of the Church are solemnly obliged to respect natural law and the teachings that have been handed down to them from their predecessors, all the way back to Christ himself.

Founded in 1865, Ave Maria Press,
a ministry of the Congregation of
Holy Cross, is a Catholic publishing
company that serves the spiritual and
formative needs of the Church and its
schools, institutions, and ministers;
Christian individuals and families; and
others seeking spiritual nourishment.

For a complete listing of titles from

Ave Maria Press

Sorin Books

Forest of Peace

Christian Classics

visit www.avemariapress.com

ave maria press® / Notre Dame, IN 46556
A Ministry of the Indiana Province of Holy Cross